WALDSTADION

Herausgeber / *Publisher*: Bernard Bol

Konzeption und Realisation / *Concept, art direction*: Peter Flachmann

Redaktion / *Edited by*: Dr. Peter Lempert, Hannah Lea

Fotos / *Photographs*: Mads Madsen, Erwin Schlegelmilch (S. 6), Gundhard Marth (S. 10/11), Jochen Keute (S. 26/27), Alexander Haselhoff (S. 28)

Foodstyling / *Foodstyling*: Michael Kuper

Kochstudio / *Recipes*: Stephanie Rilling

ISBN 3-92 46 78-32-4

Frankforter

Ein Kochbuch für »Frankfurter«-Fans
von Bernard Bol
mit Fotos von Mads Madsen

A cookery book for «Frankfurter» fans,
by Bernard Bol
with photos by Mads Madsen

ZABERT
SANDMANN

Römer-Bembel
POSSMANN
Frankfurter
Äpfelwein

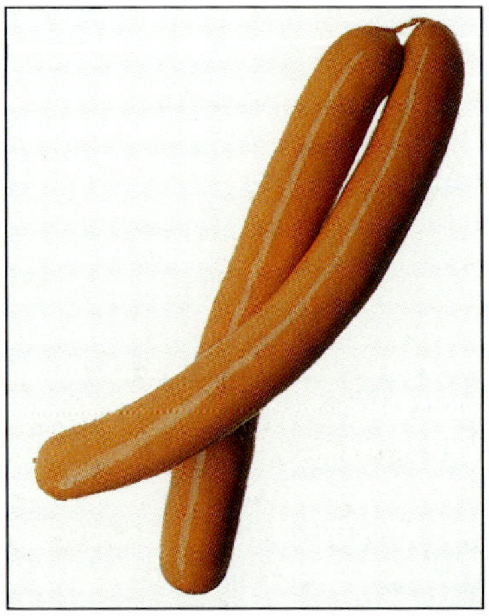

Sie treten nur paarweise auf, sind knackig, schlank, von einem zarten Rauchgeschmack umgeben und kennen keine sozialen Unterschiede. Ihre Popularität geht durch alle Gesellschaftsschichten, man findet sie in der Würstchenbude ebenso wie in manchem Grand Hotel. Ein demokratisches Zwillingspaar, so könnte man die Frankfurter Würstchen nennen. Es gibt auf der Welt viele Freunde dieser Spezialität, denen dieses Buch gewidmet ist. Es befaßt sich mit der Geschichte der Würstchen und deren Vielseitigkeit als kleine kulinarische Köstlichkeit und Abwechslung.

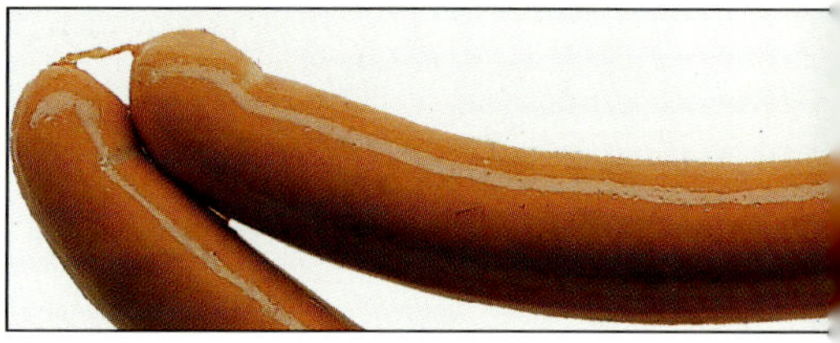

Nach dem Motto: Würstchen hat man immer im Hause – was könnte man damit schnell zaubern?

Viel Spaß bei der Zubereitung – auf daß auch Sie bald ein »Frankfurter«-Fan sind, sofern nicht schon längst geschehen!

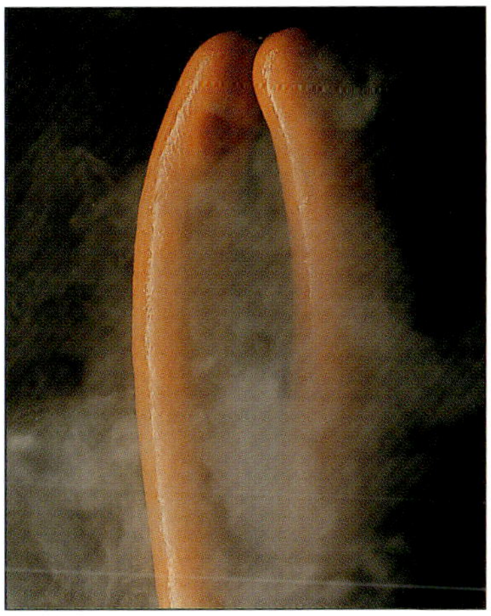

They only come in pairs – they're slim, juicy and have a delicate smoked taste. They break every class barrier and are just as at home at a hot dog stand as at the Grand Hotel. Frankfurter sausages – truly democratic twins! This unique speciality has many friends and fans right around the globe, and it is to these people that this book is dedicated. It details the history of Frankfurter sausages and gives an insight into the versatility of this culinary delicacy. And versatile they are: with a can of sausages in your kitchen cupboard, you'll always be able to spirit up a tasty dish at a moment's notice.

Happy cooking – in the hope that you, too, will soon be a confirmed «Frankfurter»-fan . . . if you aren't already!

»Frankfurter Römer« mit dem Gerechtigkeitsbrunnen

«Frankfurt Römer» with fountain of justice

Die »Frankfurter« gestern

»Original Frankfurter« – nur gebraten

Der Frankfurter Chronist Achilles August Lersner weist eine Beschreibung dieser Spezialität aus der stolzen alten Reichsstadt am Main schon für das Jahr 1487 nach. Das bedeutet ebensowenig einen fest datierbaren »Geburtstag«, noch heißt es, daß sie vorher in Frankfurt unbekannt waren. Zu diesem Zeitpunkt treten die Frankfurter Bratwürste vielmehr lediglich für uns Nachgeborene aus dem Dunkel ihrer Geschichte heraus. Doch damals wiesen sie ein anderes Innenleben auf als heutzutage. Sie waren mit Brat oder Brät gefüllt, worunter man eine mettähnliche Füllung versteht.

Der Frankfurter General Anzeiger schreibt in einem Artikel am 4. Februar 1938: »Die Frankfurter Würstchen zählen zu den Merkwürdigkeiten unserer Stadt. Der Name unserer Stadt sei weniger durch Goethe als durch die Würstchen bekannt geworden. Geburt um 1500. Die Freilegung des Karmeliterklosters hat im Speisesaal an einer Fenstersäule ein paar Frankfurter Würste in treuer Kameradschaft mit einem Boxbeutel zu Tage gebracht.«

Die Wiege der typischen geräucherten »Frankfurter« stand im alten Frankfurter Metzgerviertel zwischen Dom und Römerberg. Hier im »Worschtquartier« genannten Bezirk hatten die Metzger traditionsgemäß ihre Stände, im Volksmund »Schirne« genannt.

Schilderungen von Chronisten zufolge waren die »Frankfurter« selbst bei illustren Anlässen wie Kaiserkrönungen vertreten. Bei der Krönung Kaiser Maximilian II. im Jahre 1592 war der auf dem Römerberg am Spieß gebratene Ochse, der vor den Augen des Kaisers angeschnitten wurde, »gespickt und ausgefüllt gewesen mit allerhand Thieren als einem Schwein, Hammel, Reh, etliche Spanferkeleien, Antvogeln, Rephünern, Pfauen, Crematsvögeln, Gänsen, Enten, Hühnern, Hanen und Bratwürsten«.

Goethe schildert in Dichtung und Wahrheit, daß bei den Krönungsfeierlichkeiten von Joseph II. im Jahre 1764 am Roßmarkt vor dem Hause des Krönungsbotschafters Fürst Esterhazy Brot und Würste unter das Volk verteilt worden seien. Leider fehlt der Beweis dafür, ob es Frankfurter Bratwürste gewesen waren.

Doch die geschäftstüchtigen Mainstädter sahen dies nicht ganz so eng und tauften ihre »Frankfurter« — einfach »Krönungswürste« — eine Bezeichnung, die sich lange Zeit gehalten hat. 1749 wurde das erste Rezept für Frankfurter Bratwürste in einem Werk mit dem umständlichen Titel: »Aufrichtige und bewerte Nachrichten von allem ersinnlichen Koch- und Backwerk« niedergeschrieben: »Nehme das Fleisch von den vorderen Schenkeln des Schweines oder sonst das zarteste Fleisch und koche es mit beliebigem Speck klein, thue es in eine tiefe Schüssel,

Im »Worschtquartier« des alten Frankfurt
In the old Frankfurt «Sausage Quarter»

«Frankfurters» yesterday

«Original Frankfurters» – fried only

The Frankfurt chronicler Achilles August Lersner records a description of Frankfurters, the speciality of the majestic old city on the river Main, dating back to 1487. This is not necessarily the «birth year» of Frankfurter sausages, and nor does it mean that they were unknown in Frankfurt before this date. It is at this time, however, that Frankfurter sausages first appear in recorded history. In those days, they had different ingredients than they do today, and were filled with a different type of sausage meat.

Krönung Joseph II. im Jahre 1764, Krönungsmahl im Kaisersaal
Coronation of Joseph II in 1764, coronation feast in the Emperor's Hall

A Frankfurt newspaper reported in 1938: «The Frankfurt sausage is one of the curiosities of our city. The name of our city has achieved worldwide fame — thanks not to Goethe, but to our sausages. Birth: around 1500. Indeed, excavations of the refectory in the Carmelite monastery have revealed a couple of Frankfurt sausages in a window column, ensconced throughout the centuries in loyal fellowship with an empty wine bottle.»

The official birthplace of the typical smoked «Frankfurters» is thought to be the old Frankfurt butchers' quarter between the cathedral and the Römerberg. The area was in fact titled «sausage quarter», as by tradition, the butchers used to have their stands here and sell their wares to the population.

Contemporary reports indicate that Frankfurter sausages were even present at illustrious occasions such as the coronations of German Emperors. At the coronation of Maximilian II in 1592, the spit-roasted ox was ceremoniously sliced open in front of the new Emperor's eyes, revealing «a larding and stuffing of meats from all kinds of animals — pork, mutton, venison, suckling pig, partridge, peacock, goose, duck, chicken, cockerel and sausage.»

Goethe also records that, at the coronation celebrations of Joseph II in 1764, bread and sausages were distributed among the people gathered at the old horse market, in front of the house of the coronation ambassador Prince Esterhazy. Unfortunately, there is no way of knowing if the sausages were Frankfurters!

The people of the city, who had a canny eye for business, were not too particular about the facts, and were quick to christen their Frankfurters «coronation sausages» — a name which remained standard for many years. In 1749, the first recipe for Frankfurter sausages appeared in written form — in a book with the somewhat cumbersome title of «Honest and proven new recipes for all works of cooking and baking». The recipe runs as follows: «Take the meat from the front legs of the pig, or otherwise the tenderest of meat, and cook it up together with fatty bacon. Then put the mixture into a deep bowl, add various seasonings, to wit: nutmeg, mace, salt, pepper, thyme and marjoram, and add a pinch of coriander if to taste.»

Up until the beginning of the nineteenth century, Frankfurter sausages were always fried. «Fry them always, no matter what their composition», wrote Christiane Werner in her «Frankfurt Household Cookbook» of

würze es mit Muskatennuß, Muskatenblüth, Salz, Pfeffer, Thymian und Majoran, auch wann's beliebt mit Koriander». Diese Masse, auch Brät genannt, gab der Wurst den Namen Bratwurst.

Bis zum Anfang des 19. Jahrhunderts wurden die »Frankfurter« nur gebraten. Ob »Soucißchen«, »Reißwurst« oder Bratwurst – alles gebraten, schreibt Christiane Werner 1805 in ihrem »Frankfurter Koch- und Haushaltsbuch«. Die Bezeichnung »Frankfurter Würstchen« muß außerhalb der Stadt geboren worden sein. Noch um die Wende zum 19. Jahrhundert war dieser Begriff in Frankfurt nicht gebräuchlich, hier bestellte man einfach die »derr Bratwurscht« (dünne Bratwurst) oder »die Werschtscher«.

Die Wiener Konkurrenz

Eine Konkurrenz kam im Jahr 1805 aus Österreich, als in Wien die Würstchen kopiert wurden und als »Wiener Frankfurter Würstl« auf den Markt kamen. Johann Georg Lahner, geboren am 13. August 1772 in Gasseldorf Nr. 49 (Pfarre Ebermannstadt, Bistum Bamberg) in Oberfranken, hatte in Frankfurt am Main seine Metzgerlehre absolviert, bevor er 1798, wie viele Handwerksgesellen vor ihm, donauwärts, in die vielbesungene Kaiserstadt wanderte. Wien war damals wirklich das Herz Europas, und so mancher aus dem Reich hat es hier zu Ansehen und Wohlstand gebracht. Nach Tätigkeiten als Handlanger und Aufhackknecht bei einem Fleischhauer soll eine wohltätige Baronin Lahner ein Dahrlehen von 300 fl. Münz gewährt haben, womit er 1804 im Schottenfeld Nr. 274 eine kleine Selcherei errichtete. Im Mai 1805 erzeugte er zum ersten Mal seine »Frankfurter Würstl«, eine Wurstsorte, die bis dahin in Wien unbekannt war. Er gab den Würstlen den Namen »Frankfurter«, wohl in Erinnerung an die Stadt, in der er sein Handwerk gelernt hatte.

In einer Schrift über Lahners einstige Pfarre Ebermannstadt aus dem Jahre 1970 steht zu lesen, daß der Name »Frankfurter« nicht von der Stadt, als vielmehr von dessen Heimatland Franken abgeleitet worden sei.

Wie dem auch sei, die Frankfurter – man nannte sie bald auch den Champagner unter den Würstchen – fanden schnell Anklang bei den feinschmeckerischen Wienern, deren tägliches Gabelfrühstück mit Senf oder Kren sie namentlich wurden. Trotz vieler Nachahmungen waren die Lahnerschen Frankfurter die besten, und selbst Kaiser Franz Joseph ließ sich nicht selten für sein eigenes Frühstück ein paar heiße Lahnersche »Frankfurter« und ein Glas Bier, frisch vom Faß, vom nahe der Hofburg gelegenen Michaeler Bierhaus bringen. Ein Beleg dafür, daß die »Frankfurter« auch in Wien hoffähig waren und als Wiener Delikatesse bzw. »Wiener Würstl« auch über die Grenzen bekannt wurden.

1805, «wherein all young women receive the most expedient and understandable teaching on culinary and household matters.»

«Frankfurter sausages» the term must have originated outside the city itself. The term was still not customary in Frankfurt at the turn of the 18th century. Here, people simply ordered «thin friers» or just plain «sausages».

The Viennese competition

In 1805, the Frankfurters received some competition from Austria. The sausages were copied in Vienna and marketed as «Vienna Frankfurter Sausages». Johann Georg Lahner, born on 13th August, 1772, in Ebermannstadt in the diocese of Bamberg, Upper Franconia, was a butcher who had completed his apprenticeship in Frankfurt am Main. In 1798, he started on his travels as a journeyman to gain experience in his trade. Like many other craftsmen before him, he chose to journey up the Danube towards the famous city of Vienna. In those days, Vienna was truly the heart of Europe, and many a humble person from the Empire had found fame and riches within its walls. After spells working for various butchers along his way, during which he chopped meat and acted as general handyman, Lahner is then reported to have been given a loan by a charitable Baroness, which allowed him to set up a small shop for smoked meats in 1804, at Schottenfeld number 274. In May of 1805 he created his first «Frankfurter sausages», a completely new type of sausage by Viennese standards. He gave his creation the name «Frankfurters» — perhaps in honour of the city in which he had learnt his trade.

Johann Georg Lahner

A 1970 chronicle of Lahner's home town, Ebermannstadt, offers an alternative solution. The suggestion here is that the name «Frankfurters» does not stem from the city of Frankfurt but from the name of Lahner's home region — Franconia.

Whatever the truth is, the Frankfurters — they also came to be called the «champagne of sausages» — soon found popularity with the discerning Viennese, who ate them for breakfast with mustard or horse radish. In spite of many attempts at imitation, Lahner's Frankfurters remained the best, and even the Emperor Franz Joseph himself would often order a pair of piping-hot Lahner Frankfurters for breakfast, accompanied by a glass of beer, fresh fom the barrel, brought to him from the brewery close to the palace. This is proof that «Frankfurters» had by now gained a firm stronghold in the top echelons of society, and they soon became famous as a Viennese delicacy, or as «Viennese» sausages.

»Frankfurter« im Spiegel der Kochbücher des 19. Jahrhunderts

Es versteht sich von selbst, daß Rezepte mit und um die Frankfurter Würstchen auch Eingang in die einschlägigen Kochbücher bzw. Rezeptsammlungen fanden. So ist beispielsweise im »Universallexikon« der Kochkunst aus der Mitte des 19. Jahrhunderts zu lesen:

»Frankfurter Würstchen,

1/2 Kilogramm mageres Schweinefleisch von der Schulter wird mit 90 Gramm rohem Speck sehr fein gehackt, mit etwas gestoßenem schwarzen Pfeffer und gestoßenem Koriander, einer Prise geriebener Muskatnuß und dem nötigen Salz, sowie einer Prise Salpeter sehr gut vermischt, mit ein wenig Rotwein angefeuchtet und in sehr sorgfältig gesäuberte Därme gefüllt, worauf man sie entweder in Butter brät oder in Wasser kocht, meistens aber erst einige Tage in den Rauch hängt, bevor man sie brät oder kocht. Häufig wird auch noch etwas in Milch geweichtes und ausgedrücktes Weißbrot mit unter das Fleisch gemischt, was indessen bei den feinen, zur Versendung bereiteten Würstchen, nicht der Fall sein darf.

Wilhelmine Rührig, jahrzehntelang Köchin bei wohlangesehenen Frankfurter Familien, behandelt in ihrem praktischen »Frankfurter Kochbuch« (1860 und 1877) die Frankfurter Würstchen wie folgt:

Wurstkuchen

Von einem Pfund Mehl, einem Viertelpfund Butter, einem Glas Wasser, etwas Salz — macht man einen Teig, den man tüchtig verarbeitet und länglich ausrollt, legt dann eine große frische Bratwurst hinein, rollt den Teig fest darum und bildet einen Kranz davon, bestreicht diesen mit einem Ei und bäckt ihn auf einem mit Mehl bestäubten Blech 3/4 Stunden in einem ziemlich heißen Ofen.

Frische Bratwurst

Dieselbe taucht man vorher in heißes Wasser, damit sie nicht platzt und läßt sie ebenfalls rasch in Butter braun braten.

Geräucherte Bratwurst

legt man in kochendes Wasser und läßt sie 10 Minuten darin ziehen. Diese braucht nicht stark, sondern nur langsam zu kochen. Die dritte Variante der Wilhelmine Rührig-Würstchen geht schon stark in die Richtung der uns heute bekannten Frankfurter Würstchen.

Henriette Davidis beschreibt in ihrem »Praktischen Kochbuch für die gewöhnliche und feinere Küche« im Jahr 1898 sogar drei verschiedene »Frankfurter«.

Frankfurter Knackwürstchen

Diese sowie Wiener und Jauersche Würstchen werden mit kochendem Wasser bedeckt, 10 Minuten zugedeckt auf eine heiße Platte gestellt und roher Meerrettich ohne weitere Zutaten dazu angerichtet. Auch geben diese Würstchen eine treffliche Beilage zu jedem Kohlgemüse oder zu Kartoffel- und Bohnensalat.

Frankfurter Bratwurst

Durchwachsenes Schweinefleisch ohne Sehnen, auch etwas Fett, wird fein gehackt, mit Salz, Muskatblüte, Koriander, wenig Pfeffer und etwas rotem Wein gewürzt und in Schweinsdärme gefüllt. Frisch ist diese Wurst am feinsten, doch auch leicht geräuchert sehr gut. Man hängt sie in der Luft auf.

Frankfurter Knoblauchwürstchen

2 Teile vom zartesten Schweinefleisch und 1 Teil Kalbfleisch aus der Keule wird zusammen gehackt, nicht zu fein, mit Pfeffer, Salz und etwas Knoblauch gewürzt. Dann gießt man einen Löffel voll fette Bouillon darüber, mischt die Masse gut, füllt sie in runde Schweins- oder Rindsdärme und bindet handlange Würste davon. Man hängt diese luftig auf, und wenn man Gebrauch davon machen will, läßt man sie in kochendem Wasser 5 Minuten sieden und ißt sie warm zum Frühstück. Sie schmecken sowohl frisch als geräuchert. Um den Würsten einen Knoblauchgeschmack zu geben, zerschneidet man einige geschälte Zehen Knoblauch, bedeckt sie in einem Glase mit gutem Branntwein oder Arrak, läßt sie mehrere Stunden anziehen und würzt damit nach Belieben stark oder schwach.

«Frankfurters» in cookery books of the nineteenth century

It is no surprise that recipes with and about Frankfurters soon graced the pages of standard cookery books and collections. For example, the «Universal Encyclopaedia of Cookery», published in the middle of the nineteenth century, contains the following recipe:

Frankfurter sausages:

$^{1}/_{2}$ kilogramme of lean pork (shoulder) is chopped finely and mixed with 90 grammes of raw bacon, some ground black pepper and ground coriander, a pinch of grated nutmeg and salt to taste, and a pinch of salpetre. Moisten the mixture with a little red wine, and stuff into the carefully cleaned intestines. The sausages can then be fried in butter or heated in water, but as a rule they are hung and smoked for a few days before being boiled or fried. A little bread, soaked in milk, can also be added to the sausage meat, but this method is not employed in the finest sausages intended for dispatch to other places.

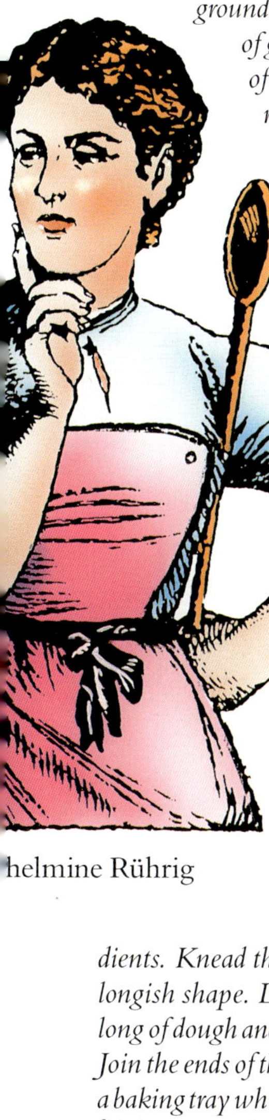

helmine Rührig

Wilhelmine Rührig, who was for many decades a cook for leading Frankfurt families, also includes a number of recipes for «Frankfurter sausages» in her «Practical Frankfurt Cookbook» (1860 and 1877):

Sausage rolls:

Take a pound of flour, a quarter pound of butter, a glass of water, some salt, and make a dough from these ingredients. Knead the prepared dough well and roll out into a longish shape. Lay a large, fresh sausage on top of the oblong of dough and roll the dough tightly around the sausage. Join the ends of the roll and brush the top with egg. Place on a baking tray which you have dusted with flour, and bake for $^{3}/_{4}$ hour in a fairly hot oven.

Fresh fried sausage:

Dip the sausage into hot water to prevent it from bursting, and then fry in butter until brown.

Smoked sausage:

Put into boiling water and let the sausage draw for ten minutes. Allow to simmer, do not boil.

The third variation given by Wilhelmine Rührig is very close to the Frankfurter sausages we know today.

Another author of the period, Henriette Davidis, describes a total of three different Frankfurters in her «Practical Cookbook for Everyday Meals and Delicacies» of 1898:

Boiled Frankfurters:

Frankfurters, or Viennese or Jauer sausages, are put into a pot with enough boiling water to cover the sausages. Cover the pot and leave to stand on a hot oven-plate for 10 minutes. Serve with raw horse radish and no further ingredients or garnishing. These sausages are also an excellent accompaniment to cabbage or to potato and bean salad.

Frying Frankfurters:

Take some lean pork, remove the tendons, but leave some fat on, chop finely and season with salt, mace, coriander, a little pepper and some red wine. Use pigs' intestines to make the sausages. This sausage tastes best when eaten fresh, but can also be hung and lightly smoked.

Garlic Frankfurters:

Take two parts of tenderest pork and one part of leg of veal. Chop up together (not too finely) and season with pepper, salt and a little garlic. Then pour a ladleful of meat stock over the chopped meats and mix well. Stuff into pigs' or cows' intestines and form sausages about the length of a hand. Hang the sausages in a well-ventilated place, and when you are ready to use them, let them simmer in boiling water for five minutes, and eat them hot for breakfast. To give the sausages a garlic taste, chop a few cloves of garlic, put into a glass and cover with good brandy or arrack, let the garlic marinate for a few hours and then add to the sausage mixture to taste.

Even these few recipes serve to illustrate the versatility of Frankfurter sausages. And we can guess at the work involved in transforming the basic ingredients into a culinary speciality for gourmet palates.

»Die Frankfurter erobert die Welt« (Etikettenabbildung der Firma Heinrich Schmidt Nachf.)

«Frankfurters conquer the world» (Reproduction of one of the labels of the Heinrich Schmidt Co.)

Der weltweite Siegeszug

Die »Krönungswürste« hatten sich bald die gastronomische Welt erobert. Karl Cäsar von Leonhard, Diplomat und Naturforscher, begegnete ihnen 1820 im Speisesaal des »Zähringer Hofes« in Baden-Baden, als »Frankfurter Soucisses«. Aus dem Jahr 1825 wurde berichtet, daß an den Tables d'hôte der ersten internationalen Hotels »Frankfurter« in kleinen Stücken als Delikatesse zu feinster Tafelmusik gereicht wurden.

Wie bei den feinen Hotelküchen fehlten die Bratwürste aus Frankfurt auch nicht auf den Tafeln der deutschen Fürsten. Als Beleg dafür gelten die handschriftlichen Überlieferungen der »Großherzogin Louise Haushaltsschule« in Baden-Baden. Daraus läßt sich die Wertschätzung für die Frankfurter Bratwürste ablesen, die zu Rebhühnern mit Sauerkraut als Beilage gegeben wurden. Ein großer Verehrer der »Königin der Würste« war auch Fürst Bismarck, der 1884 in Frankfurt weilte und auf dessen Frühstückstisch immer eine Schüssel Frankfurter Bratwürste stehen mußte.

Mitte der 90er Jahre des vorigen Jahrhunderts erhielten die Frankfurter geräucherten Bratwürste ihr endgültiges Aussehen, als die bis dahin verwendeten amerikanischen Därme durch hauchdünne Saitlinge der Kalmücken-Schafe aus Turkestan und Iran abgelöst wurden. Statt der Vier- und Fünfer-Größen (vier oder fünf Würstchen auf ein Pfund ungeräucherte Wurst) wurden jetzt, dem Drängen der Delikatess-Läden folgend, die Achter-Größen eingeführt und ausschließlich paarweise verkauft.

Ob auf Ozeanriesen, in Luxuszügen, in den Salons der Zeppeline oder in internationalen Hotels – der Siegeszug der »Frankfurter« war nicht mehr aufzuhalten. Letztlich schaffte die Haltbarmachung in Dosen den Durchbruch im Export und erlaubte eine jahreszeitenunabhängige Produktion.

Nach langwierigen Versuchen, u. a. unter Verwendung von Borsäure als Konservierungsmittel, kam man zur Haltbarmachung in Salzwasser. Wenn auch noch das Zulöten der Dosen per Hand ein

Frankfurters conquer the globe

Coronation sausages were soon a culinary delicacy all over the world. The diplomat and scientist Karl Cäsar von Leonhard was introduced to them in 1920 in the dining room of the Zahring Hotel in Baden-Baden. Here, they were titled «Frankfurter Soucisses». And a chronicle of 1825 reports that the tables d'hôte of first class international hotels were by this time also serving small pieces of «Frankfurter» as a delicacy — accompanied by suitably genteel musical entertainment.

Frankfurt sausages were not only part of the cuisine at the finest hotels — by this time they also featured on the banquet tables of the German nobility, as recorded in the handwritten chronicles of the Grand Duchess Louise School of Domestic Arts in Baden-Baden. The chronicles verify the popularity and status of the Frankfurter sausages, which were served as a side dish to partridges and accompanied by sauerkraut. Another great lover of the «queen of sausages» was Count Bismarck, who stayed in Frankfurt in 1884. During his sojourn, his breakfast table is reported to have been graced by a bowl of Frankfurter sausages every day.

By the mid eighteen-nineties, the Frankfurt smoked sausages had attained their present-day appearance. American-produced skins were replaced by much thinner skins, obtained from sheep from Turkestan and Iran. The size of the sausages changed, too. Up to that time there had been four or five (unsmoked) sausages to the pound, but, under pressure from the delicatessen shops the producers started making much smaller sausages, with eight to the pound. The sausages were sold only in pairs.

Whether on ocean liners, on pullman trains, in the lounges of Zeppelin airships or in international hotels — the progress of Frankfurter sausages was by now unstoppable. The final breakthrough in overseas exports came with the technique of preserving the sausages in tins. And thanks to the new canning techniques, the sausages could now be produced even at the height of summer without suffering any ill effects.

The canning techniques underwent many difficult trials before a solution was found. First attempts involved boric acid, but finally scientists hit upon the idea of using brine to conserve the sausages. Closing the cans still

Problem darstellte, konnten auf der allgemeinen Ausstellung für Volksernährung, Kochkunst, Konditorei und Gastwirtschaftsbedarfsgegenstände, die vom 3. bis 7. November 1887 in der städtischen Turnhalle zu Düsseldorf stattfand, die ersten Bratwurst-Konserven angeboten werden.

Auf der Weltausstellung in Chicago im Jahre 1883 errangen die Frankfurter eine »höchste Auszeichnung«. Von Chicago aus drang der Ruhm über den ganzen nordamerikanischen Kontinent, und bald waren die Frankfurter in jedem Delikatess-Laden erhältlich. Von nun an durften sie auf keiner einschlägigen Ausstellung fehlen: 1894 Ausstellung der Deutschen Landwirtschaftsgesellschaft in Berlin — Erster Preis; 1894 in Dresden — Goldene Medaille; 1895 in San Francisco — Höchste Auszeichnung; 1895 Ausstellung für Kochkunst, Konditorei, Bäckerei und verwandte Branchen, Frankfurt — Höchste Auszeichnung; 1900 Weltausstellung, Paris — Mit großem Erfolg; 1900 1. Internationale Kochkunstausstellung, Frankfurt — Mit großem Erfolg.

presented certain difficulties, as each tin had to be soldered and sealed by hand, but at the «General Exhibition for Nutrition, Gastronomy, Confectionery and Catering», held from 3rd to 7th November, 1887, in Düsseldorf, producers were able to exhibit the very first tinned sausages.

At the world exhibition of 1883 in Chicago, the Frankfurter sausages were given highest awards. From Chicago, their fame spread across the whole of North America, and Frankfurter sausages were soon available in every delicatessen. From this time on, they were represented at every major exhibition: 1894 Exhibition of German Agricultural Association in Berlin — first prize; 1894 in Dresden — gold medal; 1895 in San Francisco — highest award; 1895 Exhibition of gastronomy, confectionery, baking and related branches in Frankfurt — highest award; 1900 World exhibition in Paris — a resounding success; 1900 1st international culinary arts exhibition in Frankfurt — a resounding success.

Die amtlichen »Frankfurter«

Der »Stolz« der Frankfurter Schweinemetzger hatte weltweit nicht nur Bewunderer sondern auch Neider gefunden. Bis zum Ersten Weltkrieg hielten sich die versuchten »Frankfurter-Kopien» in Grenzen. Dann aber, nach der Restriktion des Krieges und der Inflation, florierte das »Frankfurter«-Geschäft ab Ende 1923 wieder. Klar, daß man da auch im Ausland nicht untätig blieb. Mit allen erdenklichen Mitteln wurden minderwertige Nachahmungen produziert; mal als »Wiener«, mal als »Hot-Dog«, mal als »Francforter« auf den Markt gebracht. Die Bezeichnung »Frankfurter Würstchen« allerdings durfte schon damals in den USA laut «Regulation Governing the Meat Inspection» nur das Erzeugnis tragen, welches im Wirtschaftsgebiet Frankfurt am Main hergestellt wurde.

Nachdem auch Roßschlächter ihre Würstchen »Frankfurter« nannten, schlossen sich die Produzenten des Originals zum Verband der Hersteller Frankfurter Würstchen e. V. zusammen. Im Jahr 1929 wurde dann amtlich, was es mit der Beschreibung »Frankfurter Würstchen« auf sich hat. Der 10. Zivilsenat des Kammergerichtes in Berlin beschloß am 28. September 1929, daß die Bezeichnung »Frankfurter Würstchen« eine Herkunftsbezeichnung ist. Demnach haben die im Wirtschaftsbezirk Frankfurt am Main herstellenden Fabrikanten alleine das Recht, ihre Erzeugnisse »Frankfurter Würstchen« zu nennen, vorausgesetzt, die strengen Vorschriften über die Zusammensetzung und Verarbeitung werden genau eingehalten. Dieses rechtskräftige Urteil wurde vom BGH am 13. Dezember 1955 bestätigt.

The official Frankfurters

The «pride» of the Frankfurt pork butchers evoked not only admiration, but also some bad feeling and envy around the world. Attempted «Frankfurter» copies were not widespread in the time leading up to the first world war. During the war, there was, of course, a general slump in activity, but once people had got over the deprivations of war and the currency inflation, the «Frankfurter» business flourished once again. Inevitably, foreign producers had not been idle. Inferior imitations appeared on the market, with all kinds of adventurous ingredients — sometimes titled «Viennese sausage» sometime «hot dog sausage», sometimes «Francforter». Yet even at that time, meat inspection regulations in the USA ensured that only sausages produced in the Frankfurt am Main area in Germany could rightfully be called «Frankfurter sausages».

The final straw came when horse butchers also started selling their sausages as «Frankfurters». The producers of the originals then took action, setting up the «Frankfurter Sausage Manufacturers Association». An official ruling on the term «Frankfurter sausage» was finally made in 1929. On 28th September 1929, the 10th civil court of appeal of the Supreme Court in Berlin ruled that the term «Frankfurter sausages» was a «designation of origin». In other words, producers in the region of Frankfurt have the sole right to call their products «Frankfurter sausages» — provided, of course, that manufacturers adhere to the strict regulations governing the composition of the products and processing. This ruling was upheld by the Federal Supreme Court on 13th December 1955.

Abb. aus den Frankfurter Nachrichten vom 13.11.1927

Picture from a Frankfurt newspaper of 13.11.1927

Die Trommel ruft, der Kriegsruf gellt,
Erschtaunt ganz Frankfort horcht,
Die Mezter-Innung zieht ins Feld,
„Jetzo geht es um die Worscht!

Die ächte Frankforter for uns!
Zu lang ham mer gekuscht,
Unn zugeguckt, wie Hinz und Kunz
Ins Handwerk uns gepuscht!

In Amsterdam, Paris unn Wien,
In Brooklyn unn uff Sylt,
Korz, wo nor steht e Worschtmaschin
Werd „Frankforter" gefillt!

Wo nor e Mezter in der Welt
Flääsch, Mehl unn Wasser mengt,
Als „Frankforter" for dheier Geld,
Hot er derrsch uffgehängt!

Den Zustand hawwe mer jetzt satt,
Jetzt werd defor gesorgt,
Daß kääner mehr der Vadderstadt
Ihr'n gute Name borgt!

In Zukunft wer'n se nach Rezept
Allää hier hergestellt,
Hier werd der Kunne net geneppt,
Er kricht was for sei Geld!

Macht sonst nor Worscht, so viel ihr kennt,
Des geht uns gar nix aan,
Was „Echte Frankforter" mer nennt,
Die mache mir allaa!

Drumm uff zum Kampf, die Fahne fliegt,
Fließt Blut, dann is uns wohl,
Mir wanke net, bis mer gesiegt
Um Frankforts Monopol!

Kuriositäten um die Würstchen

Das Neu-Isenburg Syndrom:

Während die Würstchen nachweislich ihren Ursprung in dem Frankfurter »Worschtquartier« hatten, werden diese heute nur noch in Neu–Isenburg hergestellt. 1860 gründete der Frankfurter Säumetzger Georg Adam Müller den ersten Neu–Isenburger–Würstchenbetrieb aus rein privaten Gründen. Er hatte anfangs schwer zu kämpfen und arbeitete mit einer Frankfurter Deckadresse, weil die auswärtige Kundschaft nur Bratwurst aus Frankfurt annehmen wollte. 1877 folgte Wilhelm Luft, der seine Würstchen über die Delikatessfirma Türck und Pabst, Frankfurt am Main, vertrieb und später auch die Wurstfabrik Hans Wirth nach Neu–Isenburg.

Bis zum Ersten Weltkrieg hatte sich Neu–Isenburg mit den Orten Sprendlingen, Langen und Großzimmern zum Hauptherstellungsort der Frankfurter Würstchen entwickelt. Heute werden in Frankfurt keine Frankfurter Würstchen mehr produziert, die drei konzessionierten Firmen sitzen alle in Neu–Isenburg.

Würstchen »hoch zu Kamel«:

Der Überseeversand der »Frankfurter« hatte erst nach der Weltausstellung in Chicago 1893 begonnen. Bis zum Beginn des Ersten Weltkrieges wurden Hunderttausende von Dosen über den Atlantik geschickt und etablierten einen festen Qualitätsbegriff. Asien, Südamerika, Australien und Afrika folgten. Durch die Wüsten Asiens und Afrikas mußten Kamele als Transportmittel eingesetzt werden, um die Frankfurter an ihre Bestimmungsorte zu bringen. Deshalb hatte man versucht, die Würstchen in eckigen Dosen zu verpacken, in der Annahme, daß sie dann bequemer von Kamelen getragen werden konnten. Nachdem die positive Resonanz von seiten der Kamele ausblieb, wurde wieder auf die heute noch benutzten runden Dosen zurückgegriffen.

Oddities and curiosities

The New-Isenburg syndrome

Even though the sausages can be proved to originate from the Frankfurt «sausage quarter», nowadays, they are in fact only produced in New Isenburg. In 1860, the Frankfurt pork butcher Georg Adam Müller set up the first New Isenburg sausage-making factory, solely for private reasons. Müller had a hard battle at first, and had to work under a Frankfurt cover address, as customers from outside the region would only buy sausage if it came from Frankfurt. In 1877, he was joined in New Isenburg by Wilhelm Luft, who sold his produce via the delicatessen company Türck and Pabst of Frankfurt. Later, the Hans Wirth sausage factory also settled in the area.

By the start of the first world war, New Isenburg, along with the villages of Sprendlingen, Langen and Grosszimmern, had become established as the main production centre of Frankfurter sausages. Nowadays, no Frankfurter sausages are actually produced in Frankfurt. The three companies with an official franchise are all located in New Isenburg.

Sausages on camels

Overseas exports of «Frankfurters» did not commence until after the world exhibition of 1893 in Chicago. But by the start of the first world war, hundreds of thousands of cans had been transported across the Atlantic, and the sausages had become established as a quality delicacy. Exports to Asia, South America, Australia and Africa followed. The sausages had to be transported through the deserts of Asia and Africa by camel — and so attempts were made to pack the sausages in four-cornered tins, assuming that the camels would find it easier to transport the cans if they were this shape. However, the camels failed to give the new shape their seal of approval, and so the traditional round tins came back into use as we know them today.

Frankfurter oder Wiener:

Das Verwirrspiel der »Wiener Frankfurter« ging so weit, daß 1881 auf der Patent- & Musterschutz-Ausstellung die alteingesessene Frankfurter Binding Brauerei »Wiener Würstchen« mit rohgeriebenem Meerrettich als Zwischenmahlzeit servieren ließ. Dies jedenfalls berichtete ein Frankfurter Metzgermeister in seinen Erinnerungen an Emerich Reeck im Jahre 1939.

Würstchen militant:

Auf der Umschlagseite der »Lustigen Blätter« von 1905 war ein Bild von H. Fritsch zu sehen, das die Achselklappen einer Uniform zeigt. Anlaß war die Verleihung des Namens Frankfurt an das zweite hessische Feldartillerieregiment Nr. 63. Der humorvolle Vorschlag zeigt den Anfangsbuchstaben der Stadt umgrenzt von ein Paar Frankfurter Würstchen und darüber als sinnvoller Knopf ein geöffnetes Näpfchen mit Senf. Bei diesem verlockenden Anblick lief dem braven Kanonier das Wasser im Munde zusammen.

Frankfurters or Viennese sausages?

The «Viennese Frankfurter» enigma even confused the inhabitants of Frankfurt. In fact, at the Patent and Trademark exhibition of 1881, an old-established Frankfurt brewery served its guests «Viennese sausages» as a snack with freshly-grated horse radish. At least, this is what was reported by a Frankfurt butcher to Emerich Reeck in 1939, who chronicled the events.

Militant sausages:

In 1905, the name «Frankfurt» was given to the second Hessian field artillery regiment No. 63. The occasion gave rise to some humour. The cover page of a magazine of the same year displays a picture of the epaulettes of an army uniform. The artist's humorous suggestion shows the first letter of the name of the city, tastefully framed by a pair of sausages and topped by a pot of mustard. This tempting sight made the good artilleryman's mouth water.

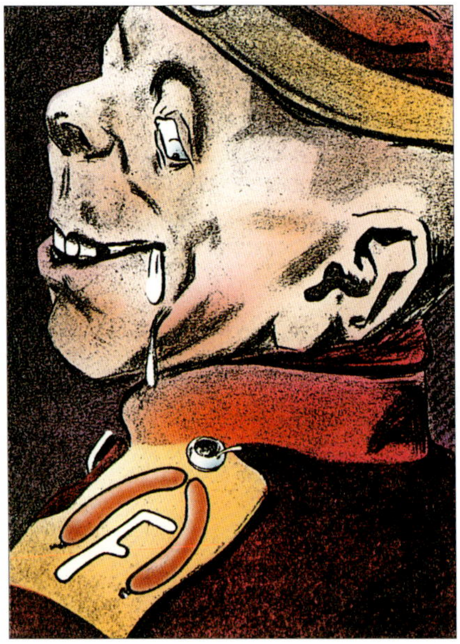

Gebrauchs-Anweisung.

Die Würstchen sind zum Genuss fertig. Der Wohlgeschmack derselben erhöht sich sehr, wenn man sie 7—10 Minuten in siedendem Wasser erwärmt. Sollen solche in der Dose heiss gemacht werden, so lege man dieselbe 1/2 Stunde in siedendes Wasser und öffne sie vorsichtig. Geschlossen erhitzte Dosen spritzen.

Directions:

Tin to be put unopened into boiling water for thirty minutes and sausages to be carefully taken out afterwards. When served with sauerkraut or potatoe salad or eaten with bread and butter they make a most delicious lunch. Closed heated tins spirts. Caution in opening.

Gebrauchsanweisungs-Text auf einem Etikett
der Firma Heinrich Schmidt Nachf. (im Jahre 1912)
Instructions an a label of the Heinrich Schmidt Co. 1912)

Die Skyline von Frankfurt
mit Blick auf den Main
und die »Alte Brücke«

The skyline of Frankfurt with a view of the river Main and the «Old Bridge»

Die »Frankfurter« Heute

Das Besondere der original Frankfurter Würstchen

Die Produktion der »Frankfurter Würstchen« unterliegt heute strengsten Reglementierungen.

1. Sie dürfen nur in Spitzenqualität im Wirtschaftsgebiet Frankfurt am Main hergestellt werden (Rechtsspruch aus dem Jahre 1929)

2. Es wird nur 100 % bestes Schweinefleisch von gut ausgereiften Mastschweinen verarbeitet, insbesondere Schinkenfleisch.

3. Das entsehnte und von Fett befreite Schinkenfleisch wird in speziellen Feinkuttern zerkleinert und nach altem Rezept fein gewürzt, ohne chemische Zusätze.

4. Die Wurstmasse wird in zarte Natursaitlinge (Schafdärme) gefüllt und nach einem besonderen, recht aufwendigen System pikant geräuchert. Hierdurch erhalten die Frankfurter Würstchen den typischen Aalrauchgeschmack.

5. Frankfurter Würstchen werden in zwei Arten angeboten: Rauchfrisch in Folie vacuumverpackt und als Konserve in Dosen — aber immer paarweise.

Drei Firmen haben heute die Lizenz, »Original Frankfurter Würstchen« zu produzieren.

«Frankfurters» Today

The unique attributes of original Frankfurter sausages

The production of «Frankfurter sausages» is nowadays subject to the most stringent regulations.

1. *They must be manufactured in the Frankfurt am Main area and must comply with highest quality standards (court ruling of 1929).*

2. *The sausages may consist solely of 100 % best pork — especially leg meat — from well-fattened pigs.*

3. *The meat is freed from fat and tendons, then chopped in special mincing machines and seasoned according to traditional recipes. No chemical additives may be used.*

4. *Natural skins (sheep's intestines) are then filled with the sausage meat. The sausages are smoked in an extremely complex process. It is this process that gives the Frankfurter sausages their typical smoked-eel taste.*

5. *Frankfurter sausages are sold in two forms: freshly-smoked and vacuum-packed in clear film, or as tinned preserves. Either way — they are only sold in pairs!*

Nowadays, three companies are licensed to produce «original Frankfurter sausages».

Grundsätzliche Zubereitung und Eßweise der Original Frankfurter Würstchen

Wasser, unter Verwendung des Salzwassers der Dose, zum Kochen bringen, von der Flamme nehmen.

Die Würstchen in das heiße Wasser legen und acht bis zehn Minuten darin ziehen lassen (nicht zudecken und nicht mehr aufkochen).

Mit mittelscharfem Senf oder frisch geschabtem Meerrettich und einer Semmel oder einer Scheibe Graubrot servieren.

How to prepare and eat original Frankfurter sausages

First put some water in a pan, and add the brine from the tin. Bring the water to the boil and then remove from the heat.

Put the sausages into the hot water and let them stand for around eight to ten minutes (do not cover and do not return to the heat).

The sausages should be served with medium-hot mustard or freshly grated horse radish and a bread roll or slice of firm brown bread.

Original Frankfurters are always served in pairs. You eat them with your fingers — never with a knife and fork!

Die Original Frankfurter Würstchen kommen nur paarweise und werden mit der Hand gegessen.
Dazu schrieb der Frankfurter Mundartdichter Stoltze:

So e Bratworscht muß indesse
Jeder ohne Gawel esse;
Nor die rechte Hand und linke
Sin als Gawel mit finf Zinke
noch gestatt — und des is gut,
weil sich kaans da steche duht.

Un die Parrer un Soldate,
Mediziner, Advokate,
Owerlehrer und Professer,
Stadtamtmänner und Assesser,
Un der ganze Handelsstand
Frißt sei Wörschtche aus der Hand.

Un die Ratsherrn und die Richter,
un die Mahler un die Dichter,
Komponiste, Journaliste,
Apotheker un Drogiste,
Und Student und Komedjant
Frißt sei Wörschtche aus der Hand.

Eine kulinarische Verwandlung

Von den vielbesungenen »armen kleinen Würstchen« kann bei den »Original Frankfurtern« wahrlich nicht gesprochen werden. Denn schon gewissermaßen »natur« verspeist sind sie eine kleine Delikatesse. Zudem sind sie das entscheidende Grundprodukt für eine ganze Reihe von pfiffigen, hier nachzulesenden Rezepturen, die aus den »Frankfurtern« eine Gaumenschmeichelei auch für Feinschmecker werden lassen.

A culinary transformation

Sausages – original Frankfurters, at least – are by no means the «poor relations» of European cuisine. Even eaten plain, without garnishing, they're a real delicacy. And they're also a basic ingredient for the range of interesting recipes we've assembled in this book, enabling you to transform simple Frankfurters into dishes which will tempt even the most discerning palate!

Originalbeilage

Kartoffelsalat

800 g kleine festkochende Kartoffeln
(vorzugsweise Sorte Gerlinde)
100 g Zwiebeln
Salz, Pfeffer, Muskat
0,2 l Fleischbrühe
500 g saure Sahne
1 Bund Schnittlauch
1 - 2 TL Essig

1. Kartoffeln waschen, garen, abpellen und etwas abkühlen lassen. Zwiebeln fein würfeln, die abgekühlten Kartoffeln in dünne Scheiben schneiden und mit den Zwiebeln und den Gewürzen vermischen.

2. Mit heißer Fleischbrühe und Essig übergießen und 10 Minuten in der Wärme ziehen lassen.

3. Saure Sahne glattrühren, kräftig würzen, den feingeschnittenen Schnittlauch einrühren, die Sauce mit dem Kartoffelsalat vermengen, nachschmecken und warmgestellt einige Minuten ruhen lassen.

Rezept für 4 Personen
Zubereitungsdauer: ca. 40 Minuten

Original side dish

Potato Salad

800 g small, firm potatoes
100 g onions
Salt, pepper, nutmeg
0.2 l meat stock
500 g soured cream
1 bunch of chives
1-2 tsp vinegar

1. Wash the potatoes, boil and peel, and leave to cool slightly. Dice the onions finely, cut the cooled potatoes into thin slices and mix with the onions and seasoning.

2. Add the vinegar and hot meat stock to the mixture and stand in a warm place for 10 minutes.

3. Stir the soured cream until smooth, season well. Stir in the finely chopped chives and add the sauce to the potato salad. Add further seasoning to taste and leave in a warm place to marinate for a few minutes before serving.

Serves four, takes about 40 minutes to prepare.

Frankfurter Cocktailwürstchen

Frankfurter Würstchen gibt es auch als Cocktailwürstchen. Sie sind ca. 3-4 cm lang und werden wie die Frankfurter Würstchen zubereitet. Mit einem Cocktailstick oder Holzzahnstocher versehen, kann man sie warm während einer Cocktailparty herumreichen. Serviert werden sie jeweils mit einem Schüsselchen Delikatess-Senf und Ketchup zum Eintunken.

Die Frankfurter Cocktailwürstchen spießt man am besten auf einen halbierten Weißkohl, der vorher in Alufolie eingeschlagen wurde.

Zubereitungsdauer: 15 Minuten

Cocktail snacks

Frankfurter Cocktail Sausages

You can also buy Frankfurters as cocktail sausages. They are 3-4 cm long and are cooked just like the normal-sized Frankfurters. Pop the sausages onto cocktail sticks — and you have a ready-made snack to hand round at your next cocktail party. Serve with dips, such as small bowls of mustard or ketchup.

Stick the cocktail snacks into a half cabbage (wrapped in aluminium foil) to serve.

Takes 15 minutes to prepare.

Frankfurter im Blätterteig

4 Blätterteigplatten
4 Frankfurter Würstchen
1 Ei
etwas Milch

1. Die Blätterteigplatten nach Packungshinweis auftauen und jede Platte bis zur Länge eines Würstchens ausrollen.

2. Frankfurter Würstchen waschen, trockentupfen, jede Teigplatte mit einem Würstchen belegen, dieses einrollen und dann in vier gleich große Stücke schneiden.

3. Das Ei mit etwas Milch verquirlen, die eingepackten Würstchen damit bestreichen, auf ein mit Backpapier ausgelegtes Backblech setzen und bei 175 Grad 15 Minuten backen.

Variationen:

1. Den ausgerollten Blätterteig vor dem Einrollen der Würstchen mit mittelscharfem Senf bestreichen. Ansonsten wie Grundrezept.

2. Den ausgerollten Blätterteig mit etwas Wasser befeuchten, Sesamsamen darauf streuen, die Würstchen einrollen, die Rolle mit dem Ei-Milch-Gemisch bestreichen und in Sesam wälzen. Wie im Grundrezept angegeben backen.

Rezept für 8 Personen
Zubereitungsdauer: ca. 20 Minuten
(ohne Auftauzeit des Blätterteiges)

Frankfurter Sausage Rolls

4 rectangles of puff pastry
4 Frankfurter sausages
1 egg
a little milk

1. Defrost the puff pastry, following instructions on packaging. Roll out each rectangle to the length of a sausage.

2. Wash the Frankfurter sausages and dab dry. Place a sausage on each length of pastry, roll up and cut into four equal pieces.

3. Beat the egg together with a little milk and brush the tops of the sausage rolls. Place on a baking tray (covered with non-stick baking paper) and bake for 15 minutes at a temperature of 175° C.

Variations:

1. Spread medium-hot mustard on the puff pastry before you form the sausage rolls. Then follow recipe above.

2. Moisten the puff pastry with a little water after you have rolled it out, and then scatter sesame seeds on the pastry. Form the sausage rolls, brush with egg and milk and roll in sesame seeds. Bake as stated in main recipe.

Serves eight, takes about 20 minutes to prepare (not including time for pastry to defrost).

Kaltes Frankfurter Schlemmerspießchen

1 kleiner Weißkohl
gefüllte Oliven
Cornichons
Perlzwiebeln
200 g Gouda
frischer Meerrettich
4 Paar Frankfurter Würstchen
Holzzahnstocher

1. Den Weißkohl halbieren, in Alufolie wickeln und beiseite stellen.

2. Cornichons in 1 bis 2 cm große Stücke, den Meerrettich in Scheiben schneiden und je nach Größe halbieren oder vierteln. Den Gouda in 1 cm große Würfel schneiden.

3. Gefüllte Oliven, Cornichons, Perlzwiebeln, Käsewürfel und den Meerrettich auf Holzzahnstocher stecken.

4. Die Frankfurter erwärmen, mit kaltem Wasser abspülen, in 2-3 cm große Stücke schneiden und ebenfalls auf die Zahnstocher stecken.

5. Die Spießchen so auf den Weißkohl stecken, daß er das Aussehen eines Igels erhält.

Rezept für 8 Personen
Zubereitungsdauer: 20 Minuten

Frankfurter Gourmet Snacks

1 small white cabbage
Stuffed olives
Pickled gherkins
Silverskin onions
200 g Gouda
Fresh horse radish
4 pairs of Frankfurter sausages
Cocktail sticks

1. Cut the cabbage in half, wrap in aluminium foil and put to one side.

2. Cut the gherkins into 1-2 cm lengths, slice the horse radish and cut each slice into half (or quarters if the slices are quite large). Dice the Gouda cheese to form 1 cm cubes.

3. Spear the stuffed olives, gherkins, silverskin onions, cheese cubes and horse radish on the cocktail sticks.

4. Heat the Frankfurters and then rinse in cold water. Cut into 2-3 cm lengths and spear on the cocktail sticks.

5. Stick the finished snacks into the cabbage, giving it the appearance of a hedgehog.

Serves eight, takes about 20 minutes to prepare.

Frankfurter Wurstsalat

2 Paar Frankfurter Würstchen
3 feste Tomaten
2 Gewürzgurken
100 g Mayonnaise
Joghurt
Salz, Pfeffer
1-2 TL Essig
1 kleine Knoblauchzehe

1. Die Frankfurter in feine Streifen, die Tomaten in kleine Stücke schneiden und die Gewürzgurken fein würfeln.

2. Die Mayonnaise mit etwas Joghurt vermischen, Knoblauch hineinpressen und mit Salz, Pfeffer und Essig pikant abschmecken.

3. Alle Zutaten vorsichtig miteinander vermengen und ca. 30 Minuten ziehen lassen. Nochmals abschmecken und mit Schwarz- oder Graubrot und Butter servieren.

Rezept für 2 -3 Personen
Zubereitungsdauer: 15 Minuten
(ohne die 30 Minuten Ruhezeit)

Frankfurter Sausage Salad

2 pairs of Frankfurter sausages
3 firm tomatoes
2 pickled gherkins
100 g mayonnaise
Yoghurt
Salt, pepper
Vinegar
1 small clove of garlic

1. Slice the Frankfurters into thin strips, cut the tomatoes into small pieces and dice the gherkins.

2. Mix the mayonnaise with some yoghurt, crush the garlic into the mixture and season well with salt, pepper and vinegar.

3. Gently stir all the ingredients together and allow to stand for about 30 minutes. Add further seasoning to taste, and serve with traditional black or brown bread and butter.

Serves 2-3 people, takes about 15 minutes to prepare (not including time for salad to marinate).

fred Ullmer

Frankfurter Wurstsalat mit einem Hauch Karibik

2 Bananen
1 Apfel
4 Scheiben Ananas
½ Bund Lauchzwiebeln
2 Paar Frankfurter Würstchen
1 Ei
1 TL Senf
1 TL Zitronensaft
3 EL Öl
150 g Joghurt
Salz, Pfeffer, Curry, Zucker

1. Bananen schälen und in Scheiben schneiden. Den Apfel schälen, entkernen und würfeln. Die Ananasscheiben in Würfel, die Lauchzwiebeln in Ringe und die Würstchen in Scheiben schneiden.

2. Aus Ei, Senf, Zitronensaft, Salz, Pfeffer, Curry, Zucker, Öl und Joghurt eine Soße rühren, über die vorbereiteten Zutaten gießen und ca. 1 Stunde ziehen lassen.

Rezept für 4 Personen
Zubereitungsdauer: ca. 30 Minuten
(ohne die 1 Stunde Ruhezeit)

Frankfurter Sausage Salad Caribbean Style

2 bananas
1 apple
4 pineapple rings
½ bunch of spring onions
2 pairs of Frankfurter sausages
1 egg
1 tsp mustard
1 tsp lemon juice
3 tbsp oil
150 g yoghurt
Salt, pepper, curry powder, sugar

1. Peel and slice the bananas. Peel, core and dice the apple. Dice the pineapple rings, cut the spring onions into rings and slice the sausages.

2. Mix the egg, mustard, lemon juice, salt, pepper, curry powder, sugar, oil and yoghurt to make a marinade, pour over the chopped ingredients and allow to stand for about one hour.

Serves four, takes about 30 minutes to prepare
(not including time for salad to marinate).

Salat von Frankfurter Würstchen und Käse

2 Paar Frankfurter Würstchen
100 g Gouda
1 kleine Zwiebel
2 Gewürzgurken
3 El Öl
2 El Essig
Salz, Pfeffer
Senf

1. Die Würstchen in feine Scheiben und den Käse in dünne Streifen schneiden. Die Gewürzgurken würfeln und die Zwiebel hacken.

2. Aus Öl, Essig, Salz und Pfeffer eine Salatsoße rühren, mit Senf abschmecken. Gewürzgurken und Zwiebel zugeben und über die Würstchen und den Käse geben.

3. Gut vermischt mindestens 30 Minuten ziehen lassen, nochmals abschmecken und zu Butterbrot und Bier reichen.

Rezept für 4 Personen
Zubereitungsdauer: 15 Minuten
(ohne die 30 Minuten Ruhezeit)

Frankfurter Sausage and Cheese Salad

2 pairs of Frankfurter sausages
100 g Gouda cheese
1 small onion
2 pickled gherkins
3 tbsp oil
2 tbsp vinegar
Salt, pepper
Mustard

1. Slice the sausages thinly and cut the cheese into small strips. Dice the gherkins and chop the onion.

2. Make a salad sauce from the oil, vinegar, salt and pepper, season with mustard, add gherkins and onion, and pour over the sausages and cheese.

3. Stir well and allow to marinate for at least 30 minutes. Add further seasoning to taste and serve with buttered bread and beer.

Serves four, takes about 15 minutes to prepare (not including time for salad to marinate).

Frankfurter Erbsensuppe

750 g Erbsen aus der Dose
½ l Fleischbrühe
½ l Milch
1 Bund Petersilie
50 g magerer Speck
2 Zwiebeln
1 kleine Karotte
½ Lorbeerblatt
1 Thymianzweig
1 Stange Lauch
4 Paar Frankfurter Würstchen
2 Scheiben Weißbrot
50 g Butter
50 g Mehl
Salz

1. Die abgetropften Erbsen im Mixer zerkleinern, salzen und mit heißer Fleischbrühe übergießen.

2. Suppe in einen Topf geben und unter ständigem Rühren mit einem Schneebesen die Milch hinzufügen.

3. Karotte und Zwiebeln fein würfeln. Den Speck auslassen und die Karotte und die Zwiebeln darin anschwitzen. Kleingeschnittenen Lauch, den Lorbeer, einen Petersilienstengel und Thymian zugeben, mit der Erbsensuppe aufgießen und ca. 20 Minuten kochen lassen.

4. Im Mixer pürieren.

5. Butter und Mehl in einem Topf anschwitzen, die Suppe nach und nach zugeben und aufkochen lassen.

6. Frankfurter in feine Scheiben schneiden und zu der Suppe geben.

7. Kurz vor dem Servieren mit gehackter Petersilie verzieren und in Würfel geschnittenes, geröstetes Weißbrot dazu reichen.

Rezept für 4 Personen
Zubereitungsdauer: 45 Minuten

Frankfurter Pea Soup

750 g tinned peas
½ l meat stock
½ l milk
1 bunch of parsley
50 g lean bacon
2 onions
1 small carrot
½ bayleaf
1 bunch of thyme
1 leek
4 pairs of Frankfurter sausages
2 slices of white bread
50 g butter
50 g flour
Salt

1. Drain the peas, liquidize using a mixer and add salt to taste. Pour on the hot meat stock.

2. Pour the soup into a pan and whisk in the milk.

3. Dice the carrot and onions. Gently fry bacon to render down the fat, then add the onions and carrot. Add the chopped leek, bayleaf, a stalk of parsley and the thyme. Pour the pea soup onto this mixture and allow to simmer for about 20 minutes.

4. Put the soup into a mixer and liquidize.

5. Make a roux with butter and flour, add the soup a little at a time and bring to the boil.

6. Cut the sausages into thin slices and add to the soup.

7. Garnish with chopped parsley, serve with croutons.

Serves four, takes 45 minutes to prepare.

Frankfurter Kartoffelsuppe

500 g Kartoffeln
30 g Butter
2 Stangen Lauch
4 Schalotten
1 EL Mehl
1 l Rinderbrühe
Salz, Pfeffer
Majoran
4 Paar Frankfurter Würstchen

1. Kartoffeln waschen, kochen, schälen, erkalten lassen und reiben.

2. Schalotten fein würfeln, Lauch in Scheiben schneiden und beides kurz in heißer Butter dämpfen. Mehl zugeben und aufschäumen lassen. Zur Kartoffelmasse geben.

3. Heiße Brühe aufgießen, mit Salz und Majoran abschmecken und gut durchkochen.

4. Die Frankfurter Würstchen in dünne Scheiben schneiden und hinzufügen. 5 Minuten ziehen lassen und servieren.

Rezept für 4 Personen
Zubereitungsdauer: 30 Minuten
(ohne Kochzeit der Kartoffeln)

Frankfurter Potato Soup

500 g potatoes
30 g butter
2 leeks
4 shallots
1 tbsp flour
1 l beef stock
Salt, pepper
Marjoram
4 pairs of Frankfurter sausages

1. Wash, boil and peel the potatoes. Leave to cool, then grate.

2. Dice the shallots finely, slice the leeks and fry gently in hot butter. Sprinkle on the flour, stirring thoroughly until the mixture is bubbling. Add the mixture to the potatoes.

3. Pour on the hot beef stock, season with salt and marjoram and simmer well.

4. Cut the Frankfurters into thin slices and add to the soup. Allow to simmer for a further five minutes before serving.

Serves four, takes 30 minutes to prepare
(not including time to boil potatoes).

Wurzelgemüsesuppe mit Frankfurter Würstchen

200 g Karotten
150 g weiße Rüben
150 g Petersilienwurzel
150 g Speck
1 Zwiebel
5 Nelken
1 Knoblauchzehe
1 l Fleischbrühe
250 g Erbsen
4 Paar Frankfurter Würstchen
Salz, Pfeffer
Muskat
1 Lorbeerblatt
1 Bund Petersilie

1. Karotten, weiße Rüben und Petersilienwurzel in kleine Stücke schneiden.

2. Mit 10 g Speck und der mit den Nelken gespickten Zwiebel in einen Topf geben, mit Fleischbrühe aufgießen, mit Salz, Pfeffer, Muskat, Lorbeerblatt und Knoblauch würzen und eine halbe Stunde köcheln lassen.

3. Gespickte Zwiebel und Lorbeerblatt herausnehmen und die Erbsen hinzufügen.

4. Frankfurter erwärmen, Suppe in eine Servierschüssel geben und die Würstchen hineinlegen.

5. Den restlichen Speck in mundgerechte Scheiben schneiden und dazugeben. Mit frisch gehackter Petersilie überstreuen und servieren.

Rezept für 4-5 Personen
Zubereitungsdauer: 45 Minuten

Carrot and Turnip Soup with Frankfurters

200 g carrots
150 g turnips
150 parsley root
150 g bacon
1 onion
5 cloves
1 clove of garlic
1 l meat stock
250 g peas
4 pairs of Frankfurter sausages
Salt, pepper
Nutmeg
1 bayleaf
1 bunch of parsley

1. Chop the carrots, turnips and parsley root.

2. Stick the cloves into the onion and put into a pan together with 10 g of bacon. Pour on the meat stock, and season with salt, pepper, nutmeg, bayleaf and garlic. Allow to simmer for 30 minutes.

3. Remove the onion and bayleaf and add the peas.

4. Heat the Frankfurters. Pour the soup into a serving dish and add the sausages.

5. Cut the remaining bacon into bite-sized pieces and add to the soup. Garnish with freshly chopped parsley before serving.

Serves 4-5 people, takes 45 minutes to prepare.

Linsensuppe nach Frankfurter Art

250 g Linsen
1 l Wasser
1 große Stange Lauch
100 g Sellerie
100 g Möhren
100 g Kartoffeln
Speckschwarten oder Dörrfleischreste
2 Zwiebeln
150 Dörrfleisch
1-3 EL Essig
Salz, Pfeffer
4 Paar Frankfurter Würstchen

1. Linsen in einem Sieb mit kaltem Wasser überbrausen und in einen Topf mit Wasser geben. Über Nacht einweichen.

2. Am nächsten Tag Lauch, Sellerie, Möhren und Kartoffeln putzen und waschen, in kleine Würfel schneiden und mit den Speckschwarten zu Linsen und Wasser geben. Zugedeckt bei starker Hitze zum Kochen bringen, danach ca. 30 Minuten bei schwacher Hitze köcheln lassen.

3. Dörrfleisch und Zwiebeln fein würfeln und in einer Bratpfanne unter mehrmaligem Wenden bei mittlerer Hitze braun und knusprig braten. In die Suppe rühren und ca. 10 Minuten durchziehen lassen. Mit Salz, Pfeffer und Essig abschmecken.

4. Die Frankfurter Würstchen erwärmen, in 1 cm dicke Stücke schneiden und in die Suppe geben. Die Würstchen können aber auch separat und ungeschnitten auf einem warmen Teller serviert werden.

Rezept für 4 Personen
Zubereitungsdauer: 40 Minuten

Frankfurter Lentil Soup

250 g lentils
1 l water
1 large leek
100 g celery
100 g carrots
100 g potatoes
Thick bacon rind or dried meat leftovers
2 onions
150 dried meat
1-3 tbsp vinegar
Salt, pepper
4 pairs of Frankfurter sausages

1. Put the lentils in a sieve, rinse in cold water and soak in water overnight.

2. The next day, clean and rinse the leek, celery, carrots and potatoes and dice them. Add the diced vegetables and bacon rind to the lentils and water. Bring to the boil, then simmer over a low heat for about 30 minutes.

3. Dice the dried meat and onion finely and fry over a medium heat until crispy, turning frequently. Stir into the soup and allow to stand for about 10 minutes. Season with salt, pepper and vinegar.

4. Heat the Frankfurter sausages, slice into 1 cm lengths and add to the soup. If you wish, you can also serve the sausages separately (uncut) on a warm plate.

Serves four, takes 40 minutes to prepare
(not including time to soak lentils).

Für den kleinen Hunger –
warme Snacks

Warm snacks

Sauerkrauttorte mit Frankfurter Würstchen
Sauerkraut Flan with Frankfurters

Sauerkrauttorte mit Frankfurter Würstchen

Teig:
300 g Mehl
175 g Butter
Salz
1 Ei
6 EL Wasser

Für den Belag:
500 g fertig gekochtes Sauerkraut
6 Paar Frankfurter Würstchen
0,3 l Sahne
3 Eigelb

1. Zutaten für den Teig verkneten und eine Springform (24 cm Ø) damit auslegen.

2. Das sehr gut abgetropfte Sauerkraut mit den kleingeschnittenen Würstchen vermengt in die Form füllen, mit dem Sahne-Ei-Gemisch übergießen und im vorgeheizten Backofen bei 180 Grad ca. 1 Stunde überbacken.

Rezept (als Snack) für 8-12 Personen
Zubereitungsdauer: 1 Stunde und 30 Minuten

Sauerkraut Flan with Frankfurters

Pastry:
300 g flour
175 g butter
Salt
1 egg
6 tbsp water

For the filling:
500 g ready-cooked sauerkraut
6 pairs of Frankfurter sausages
0.3 l cream
3 egg yolks

1. Mix the ingredients for the pastry together. Roll out the pastry and line a flan dish (24 cm Ø).

2. Allow the sauerkraut to drain well, then mix with chopped Frankfurters. Put the mixture into the pastry casing. Mix the egg and cream, pour on, and cook in a preheated oven (180° C) for about one hour.

Serves 8-12 people (as a snack),
takes 1 hour 30 minutes to prepare.

Frankfurter Würstchen im Lauchbett

1 kg Lauch
Salz, Pfeffer
Muskat
4 Paar Frankfurter Würstchen
0,1 l Rinderbrühe
20 g Butter

1. Den Lauch putzen und nur die unteren, weißen und hellgrünen Teile verwenden. Waschen, abtropfen und in größere Rauten schneiden. Nochmals waschen.

2. In einem Topf etwas Butter zergehen lassen, den Lauch kurz anschwitzen, mit Salz, Pfeffer und Muskat würzen. Rinderbrühe angießen und den Lauch gar dünsten.

3. Die Würstchen auf den Lauch legen und heiß werden lassen.

Rezept für 4 Personen
Zubereitungsdauer: 20 Minuten

Frankfurters with Leek

1 kg leeks
Salt, pepper
Nutmeg
4 pairs of Frankfurter sausages
0.1 l beef stock
20 g butter

1. Prepare the leeks; use only the white and light green sections and discard the rest. Wash, drain and cut diagonally into large diamond-shaped pieces. Wash once again.

2. Melt a little butter in a pan, lightly fry the leek and season with salt, pepper and nutmeg. Pour on the beef stock and simmer until the leek is cooked.

3. Lay the Frankfurters on top of the leeks and serve when the sausages are hot.

Serves four, takes 20 minutes to prepare.

Frankfurter Würstchen im Blätterteigmantel

400 g Blätterteig (tiefgekühlt)
4 Paar Frankfurter Würstchen
4 Scheiben Emmentaler Käse
Paprika, edelsüß
2 Knoblauchzehen
4 EL Senf
1 EL Öl
2 Eier

1. Den Blätterteig nach Vorschrift auftauen lassen.

2. Die Frankfurter Würstchen längs halbieren, mit Emmentaler füllen und mit Paprika bestreuen.

3. Den Blätterteig 3 mm dick ausrollen und in Rechtecke schneiden, die nicht ganz so lang sind wie die Frankfurter.

4. Knoblauch pressen, mit Senf mischen und die Würstchen damit bestreichen.

5. Jedes Würstchen so in ein Teigrechteck einrollen, daß beidseitig ca. 1 cm herausragt. Die Teigränder mit Eiweiß verschließen. Die Wurstrollen mit übrigen Teigstreifen hübsch verzieren und mit verquirltem Eigelb bestreichen.

6. Ein Backblech mit Öl bestreichen, die Würstchen darauflegen und im vorgeheizten Backofen bei 200 Grad 15-20 Minuten goldgelb backen.

Rezept für 4 Personen
Zubereitungsdauer: 30 Minuten (ohne Auftauzeit)

Frankfurters in Puff Pastry

400 g puff pastry (frozen)
4 pairs of Frankfurter sausages
4 slices of Emmental cheese
Paprika powder
2 cloves of garlic
4 tbsp mustard
1 tbsp oil
2 eggs

1. Defrost the puff pastry as indicated on the pack.

2. Cut the Frankfurters into half lengthwise, tuck a slice of Emmental cheese between the two halves and sprinkle with paprika.

3. Roll the puff pastry into 3 mm thick strips, cut into rectangles which are a little shorter than the Frankfurters.

4. Crush the garlic, mix with the mustard and coat the sausages with the mixture.

5. Roll the sausages up in the puff pastry, leaving 1 cm of sausage visible at either end. Seal the pastry roll with a little egg white. Decorate the rolls using leftover pastry strips and brush with egg yolk.

6. Brush a baking tray with oil, put the Frankfurter rolls on the tray and bake in a preheated oven (200° C) for 15-20 minutes until golden brown.

Serves four, takes 30 minutes to prepare
(not including time for pastry to defrost).

Frankfurter Ananas-Käse-Toast

2 Paar Frankfurter Würstchen
4 Scheiben Ananas
0,1 l Weißwein
4 Scheiben Emmentaler Käse
Curry
4 Scheiben Toast
Butter
4 Holzspieße

1. Würstchen und Ananas vierteln und abwechselnd auf 4 Holzspieße stecken.

2. In eine feuerfeste Form legen, Wein darübergießen, mit Curry würzen und den Käse über die Spieße legen.

3. Im Backofen übergrillen, bis der Käse Farbe zieht.

4. Auf gebutterten Toasts anrichten.

Rezept für 4 Personen
Zubereitungsdauer: 15 Minuten

Caribbean Frankfurters with Toast

2 pairs of Frankfurter sausages
4 pineapple rings
0.1 l white wine
4 slices of Emmental cheese
Curry powder
4 slices of toast
Butter
4 wooden skewers

1. Cut the sausages and pineapple into quarters and spear on four wooden skwers, alternating between sausage and pineapple pieces.

2. Put the kebabs into an ovenproof dish, pour on the wine, season with curry powder and lay the slices of cheese on top.

3. Heat in the oven until the cheese turns golden brown.

4. Serve on buttered toast.

Serves four, takes 15 minutes to prepare.

Frankfurter Schaschlik

200 g Gouda
4 mittelgroße Tomaten
100 g durchwachsener Speck
2 Paar Frankfurter Würstchen
¼ l Rinderbrühe
Paprika, edelsüß
Curry
Stangenbrot
4 Holzspieße

1. Gouda in 16 Vierecke, den Speck in 16 Scheiben schneiden. Die gewaschenen Tomaten und die Frankfurter vierteln und alles abwechselnd auf 4 Holzspieße stecken und in eine feuerfeste Form legen.

2. Spieße mit Rinderbrühe übergießen und mit Paprika und Curry bestäuben.

3. Im vorgeheizten Backofen bei 200 Grad ca. 10 Minuten garen lassen. Mit Stangenbrot servieren.

Rezept für 4 Personen
Zubereitungsdauer: 25 Minuten

Frankfurter Kebabs

200 g Gouda cheese
4 medium-large tomatoes
100 g fatty bacon
2 pairs of Frankfurter sausages
¼ l beef stock
Paprika powder
Curry powder
Baguette
4 wooden skewers

1. Cut the Gouda into 16 squares and the bacon into 16 slices. Quarter the tomatoes and sausages and make four kebabs, alternating between cheese, bacon and sausage pieces. Put the kebabs into an ovenproof dish.

2. Pour the beef stock over the kebabs and sprinkle with paprika and curry powder.

3. Cook in a preheated oven (200° C) for about 10 minutes. Serve with sliced baguette.

Serves four, takes 25 minutes to prepare.

Würstchen mit Kartoffeln Frankfurter Art

1,2 kg Kartoffeln
1 Zwiebel
50 g Butter
1 EL Mehl
½ l Fleischbrühe
4 Paar Frankfurter Würstchen
Salz, Pfeffer
Petersilie
Essig

1. Kartoffeln waschen, kochen, schälen und in Scheiben schneiden. Die Zwiebel fein hacken, in Butter anschwitzen, mit dem Mehl verrühren, danach mit Fleischbrühe auffüllen und mit Salz und Pfeffer abschmecken. Das Ganze über die Kartoffeln gießen und durchziehen lassen.

2. Frankfurter Würstchen in heißem Wasser ziehen lassen, dann in feine Scheiben schneiden und unter die Masse mischen. Ca. 10 Minuten bei schwacher Hitze ziehen lassen.

3. Nochmals abschmecken, eventuell den Essig zufügen und vor dem Servieren mit gehackter Petersilie bestreuen.

Rezept für 4 Personen
Zubereitungsdauer: ca. 30 Minuten
(ohne Kochzeit für die Kartoffeln)

Sausage and Potatoes, Frankfurter Style

1200 g potatoes
1 onion
50 g butter
1 tbsp flour
½ l meat stock
4 pairs of Frankfurter sausages
Salt, pepper
Parsley
Vinegar

1. Wash and boil the potatoes; then peel and cut into slices. Chop the onions finely, fry gently in butter. Then stir in the flour, pour on the meat stock and season with salt and pepper. Pour the mixture over the potatoes and allow to marinate.

2. Heat the Frankfurters in hot water, then cut into thin slices and add to the other ingredients. Simmer over a low heat for about 10 minutes.

3. Add further seasoning to taste, add vinegar if required. Garnish with chopped parsley before serving.

Serves four, takes about 30 minutes to prepare
(not including time to boil potatoes).

Karotteneintopf

1 kg Karotten
500 g Kartoffeln
1 Zwiebel
½ l Fleischbrühe
4 Paar Frankfurter Würstchen
Salz, Pfeffer
Zucker
3 EL Petersilie
40 g Butter
50 g Kräuterbutter
oder 125 g Crème fraîche

1. Zwiebeln fein hacken und in Butter anschwitzen. Karotten in ca. 3 cm große Stücke schneiden, zu den Zwiebeln geben und mit Brühe aufgießen. 5 Minuten köcheln lassen.

2. Kartoffeln schälen, vierteln und zugeben. Ca. 40 Minuten köcheln lassen.

3. Den Eintopf von der Herdplatte nehmen und im Mixer pürieren. Mit Salz, Pfeffer und Zucker abschmecken. Je nach Geschmack Kräuterbutter oder Crème fraîche zugeben.

4. Die Frankfurter in 1 cm große Stücke schneiden, unterrühren und erwärmen. Kurz vor dem Servieren den Karotteneintopf mit gehackter Petersilie bestreuen.

Rezept für 4 Personen
Zubereitungsdauer: ca. 1 Stunde

Carrot Soup

1 kg carrots
500 g potatoes
1 onion
½ l meat stock
4 pairs of Frankfurter sausages
Salt, pepper
Sugar
3 tbsp parsley
40 g butter
50 g herb butter
or 125 g crème fraîche

1. Dice the onions finely and fry gently in butter. Cut the carrots into 3 cm pieces, add to the onions and pour on the meat stock. Bring to the boil and simmer for 5 minutes.

2. Peel the potatoes, cut into quarters and add to the soup. Simmer for about 40 minutes.

3. Remove the soup from the heat and liquidize in the mixer. Season with salt, pepper and sugar. Add either herb butter or crème fraîche to taste.

4. Cut the Frankfurters into 1 cm pieces, add to the soup and heat. Garnish the carrot soup with chopped parsley before serving.

Serves four, takes about one hour to prepare.

Paprika-Wurst-Eintopf

150 g durchwachsener Speck
2 grüne Paprikaschoten
4 Zwiebeln
4 Paar Frankfurter Würstchen
Salz, Pfeffer
Paprika, edelsüß
1 EL Crème fraîche

1. Den Speck würfeln, die Zwiebeln klein hacken, die Paprikaschoten waschen und in Streifen schneiden.

2. Speck in einer Pfanne erhitzen, Zwiebeln zugeben und glasig dünsten. Die Paprikaschoten beifügen.

3. Etwas Wasser angießen, mit Salz, Pfeffer und Paprika würzen und die in Scheiben geschnittenen Würstchen beigeben.

4. Mit Crème fraîche abschmecken und den Eintopf auf kleiner Flamme so lange erhitzen, bis die Würstchen heiß sind.

Sausage and Pepper Stew

150 g streaky bacon
2 green peppers
4 onions
4 pairs of Frankfurter sausages
Salt, pepper
Paprika powder
1 tbsp crème fraîche

1. Dice the bacon, chop the onions. Wash the peppers and cut into strips.

2. Heat the bacon in a pan, add the onions and fry gently until transparent. Add the peppers.

3. Pour on a little water, season with salt, pepper and paprika powder. Then add the sliced sausages.

4. Add the crème fraîche to taste. Turn down the heat and simmer until the sausages are hot.

Rezept für 4 Personen
Zubereitungsdauer:
ca. 30 Minuten

Serves four,
takes about 30 minutes
to prepare.

Würstchengulasch

3 große Zwiebeln
1 EL Tomatenmark
Essig
Paprika, edelsüß
100 g Paprikawürfel (gelb, rot, grün)
100 g geschälte Kartoffeln
4 Paar Frankfurter Würstchen
¾ l Rinderbrühe
Gulaschgewürz (abgeriebene Zitronenschale, zerdrückter Knoblauch, Kümmel, Majoran)

1. Zwiebeln in feine Würfel schneiden, in etwas Fett hellbraun anschwitzen und mit Paprika und Tomatenmark würzen.

2. Mit wenig Essig ablöschen und mit Brühe auffüllen. Etwas kochen lassen, dann die Paprika und die ebenfalls gewürfelten Kartoffeln hinzufügen.

3. Frankfurter in Würfel schneiden, zum Gulasch geben, garziehen lassen und mit Gulaschgewürz abschmecken.

Sausage Goulash

3 large onions
1 tbsp tomato puree
Vinegar
Paprika powder
100 g diced peppers (yellow, red, green)
100 g peeled potatoes
4 pairs of Frankfurter sausages
¾ l beef stock
Goulash seasoning (grated lemon peel, crushed garlic, caraway, marjoram)

1. Dice the onions finely, fry gently in a little fat until golden brown and season with paprika powder and tomato puree.

2. Add a little vinegar and the beef stock. Allow to simmer for a short time, then add the peppers and diced potatoes.

3. Dice the Frankfurters, add to the goulash, allow to heat through and then add the goulash seasoning to taste.

Rezept für 4 Personen
Zubereitungsdauer:
40 Minuten

Serves four,
takes 40 minutes
to prepare.

Frankfurter Specktopf

150 g durchwachsener Speck
100 g weiße Bohnen
1 Bund Suppengrün
2 Karotten
100 g Kartoffeln
2 Paar Frankfurter Würstchen
Salz, Pfeffer
1 Lorbeerblatt
1 EL Weinessig
1 EL gehackte Petersilie

1. Die Bohnen über Nacht einweichen.

2. Karotten klein schneiden, mit dem Speck, Suppengrün und dem Lorbeerblatt zu Bohnen und Einweichwasser geben und ½ Stunde kochen. Speck, Lorbeerblatt und Suppengrün herausnehmen. Speck aufbewahren.

3. Am nächsten Tag die Bohnen zum Kochen bringen, Kartoffeln waschen, schälen, in Würfel schneiden, dazugeben und gar kochen.

4. Mit Salz, Pfeffer und Essig abschmecken. Den Speck in kleine Würfel schneiden und wieder in die Suppe geben. Die Frankfurter in Scheiben schneiden und in der Suppe erwärmen.

5. Mit Petersilie überstreuen und servieren.

Rezept für 4 Personen
Zubereitungsdauer: ca. 1 Stunde (ohne Einweichzeit)

Frankfurter Bacon Soup

150 g streaky bacon
100 g white beans
1 bunch of soup vegetables
2 carrots
100 g potatoes
2 pairs of Frankfurter sausages
Salt, pepper
1 bayleaf
1 tbsp wine vinegar
1 tbsp chopped parsley

1. Soak the beans overnight.

2. Chop the carrots, add carrots, bacon, soup vegetables and bayleaf to the beans in water and cook for 30 minutes. Remove the bacon, bayleaf and soup vegetables. Do not throw the bacon away; you will be needing it later.

3. The next day, wash, peel and dice potatoes. Bring the beans to the boil, then add potatoes and cook until soft.

4. Season with salt, pepper and vinegar. Dice the bacon finely, and add to the soup together with sliced Frankfurters. Allow to simmer until the sausages are hot.

5. Garnish with parsley before serving.

Serves four, takes about one hour to prepare
(not including time for beans to soak).

Frankfurter Gemüse-Eintopf

50 g Butter
80 g durchwachsener Speck
2 große Zwiebeln
500 g Tomaten
je 1 rote und grüne Paprikaschote
3 EL Paprika, edelsüß
1 kg festkochende Kartoffeln
½ l Fleischbrühe
Salz, Pfeffer
1 Lorbeerblatt
5 Wacholderbeeren
Kümmel
4 Paar Frankfurter Würstchen
Schnittlauch

1. Den Speck und die Zwiebeln fein würfeln und in Butter anbraten. Die gehäuteten, grob geschnittenen Tomaten zufügen. Paprikaschoten waschen, vom Kerngehäuse befreien, in Streifen schneiden und ebenfalls zugeben. Mit Paprika bestäuben.

2. Kartoffeln waschen, schälen und in große Würfel geschnitten dem Gemüse beigeben. Mit Fleischbrühe auffüllen, mit Salz, Pfeffer, Wacholderbeeren, Lorbeerblatt und Kümmel würzen und zugedeckt bei mittlerer Hitze etwa 1/2 Stunde kochen lassen. Mehrmals umrühren und eventuell etwas Wasser nachgießen.

3. Die Frankfurter in Wasser erhitzen, in 1 cm große Stücke schneiden, in den Eintopf geben und mit Schnittlauch bestreuen.

Rezept für 4 Personen
Zubereitungsdauer: ca. 1 Stunde

Frankfurter Vegetable Broth

50 g butter
80 g streaky bacon
2 large onions
500 g tomatoes
1 red and 1 green pepper
3 tbsp paprika powder
1 kg firm potatoes
½ l vegetable stock
Salt, pepper
1 bayleaf
5 juniper berries
Caraway
4 pairs of Frankfurter sausages
Chives

1. Dice the bacon and onions finely and fry gently in butter. Skin the tomatoes and cut them into large pieces, add to the bacon and onions. Wash and core the peppers, cut into strips and add to the other ingredients. Sprinkle with paprika powder.

2. Wash and peel the potatoes, cut into large cubes and add to the vegetables. Pour on the meat stock, season with salt, pepper, juniper berries, bayleaf and caraway. Cover and simmer over a medium heat for about 30 minutes. Stir frequently, adding more water if necessary.

3. Heat the Frankfurters in water, cut into 1 cm pieces, add to the broth. Garnish with chives before serving.

Serves four, takes about one hour to prepare.

Hauptgänge

Main courses

Garniertes Frankfurter Sauerkraut
Garnished Frankfurter Sauerkraut

Garniertes Frankfurter Sauerkraut

2 kg frisches Sauerkraut
2 Zwiebeln
2 Knoblauchzehen
2 EL Gänseschmalz
¼ l Apfelwein
Salz, Pfeffer
1 TL Kümmel
8-10 Wacholderbeeren
2 Nelken
ca. ½ l Wasser
600 g gepökelter Schweinehals
600 g gepökelter Schweinebauch
4 Paar Frankfurter Würstchen
4 geräucherte Mettwürstchen

1. Das frische Sauerkraut kurz in lauwarmem Wasser durchspülen und abtropfen lassen.

2. Die Zwiebeln in feine Halbringe schneiden und mit dem Gänseschmalz in einen Topf geben. Die Knoblauchzehen fein hacken und zufügen. Unter Rühren anschwitzen und mit Apfelwein ablöschen.

3. Die Hälfte des Sauerkrauts locker in den Topf schichten, sparsam salzen, reichlich pfeffern und ½ TL Kümmel, 4 Wacholderbeeren und eine Nelke hinzugeben. Mit Wasser auffüllen, bis das Kraut gerade bedeckt ist.

4. Das Fleisch auf das Sauerkraut legen und mit dem restlichen Kraut bedecken. Diese Schicht ebenfalls salzen, pfeffern und mit Wacholderbeeren, Kümmel und einer Nelke aromatisieren. Wenn nötig, wenig Wasser nachfüllen und bei geschlossenem Topf einmal aufwallen lassen. Bei geringer Hitze 80 Minuten köcheln lassen.

5. Frankfurter und Mettwürste separat in heißem Wasser garen und als Krönung auf einer mit dem Sauerkraut und dem Fleisch angerichteten Platte servieren. Dazu gehören Salzkartoffeln.

Rezept für 8 Personen
Zubereitungsdauer: ca. 2 Stunden

Garnished Frankfurter Sauerkraut

2 kg fresh sauerkraut
2 onions
2 cloves of garlic
2 tbsp goose dripping
¼ l apple wine
Salt, pepper
1 tsp caraway
8-10 juniper berries
2 cloves
½ l water (approx.)
600 g salted neck of pork
600 g salted belly of pork
4 pairs of Frankfurter sausages
4 smoked pork or beef sausages

1. Rinse the fresh sauerkraut in lukewarm water and allow to drain.

2. Cut the onions into thin half-rings, put in a pan with the goose dripping. Chop the cloves of garlic and add to the pan. Gently stir-fry the onions and then add the apple wine.

3. Put half of the sauerkraut into the pan, season with a little salt, plenty of pepper, 1 tsp caraway, 4 juniper berries and one clove. Add just enough water to cover the sauerkraut.

4. Put the meat on top of the sauerkraut and cover with the remaining sauerkraut. Season the second layer with salt, pepper, juniper berries, caraway and a clove. Add more water if necessary, cover and bring to the boil. Simmer for 80 minutes over a low heat.

5. Cook the Frankfurters and pork/beef sausages separately in hot water and serve together with the other meat on a bed of sauerkraut. Serve with boiled potatoes.

Serves eight, takes about 2 hours to prepare.

Tomatennudeln und Frankfurter Würstchen

250 g Bandnudeln
1 EL Öl
1 Zwiebel
40 g Butter
6 Tomaten
Salz
125 g Crème fraîche
4 Paar Frankfurter Würstchen
Parmesan

1. Das Öl in kochendes Salzwasser geben und darin die Bandnudeln in 9 Minuten bißfest kochen, abschrecken und gut abtropfen lassen.

2. Die Zwiebel würfeln und in Butter anschwitzen.

3. Tomaten einritzen, mit kochendem Wasser übergießen, abschrecken, enthäuten, entkernen und würfeln. Kurz mit der Zwiebel dünsten, dann die Nudeln zufügen, das Ganze gut durchschwenken und mit Salz abschmecken. Crème frache unterziehen.

4. Frankfurter in heißem Wasser garziehen lassen und in Scheiben geschnitten unter die Bandnudeln mischen. Mit geriebenem Parmesan bestreuen.

Rezept für 4 Personen
Zubereitungsdauer:
ca. 20 Minuten

Tomato Noodles with Frankfurters

250 flat noodles (Tagliatelle)
1 tbsp oil
1 onion
40 g butter
6 tomatoes
Salt
125 g créme fraîche
4 pairs of Frankfurters
Parmesan cheese

1. Add the oil to boiling, salted water and cook the noodles (about 9 minutes). Rinse under cold water and drain well.

2. Dice the onion and fry gently in butter.

3. Slit the skins of the tomatoes and pour on boiling water. Rinse under cold water, remove the skins and dice. Heat briefly with the onions, then add the noodles and stir well. Season with salt to taste and add crème fraîche.

4. Heat the Frankfurters in hot water and cut into slices. Add to the noodle mixture and sprinkle with grated Parmesan before serving.

Serves four,
takes about 20 minutes
to prepare.

Frankfurter, umwickelt mit Räucherspeck

4 kleine Äpfel
1 Zwiebel
40 g Butter
500 g Sauerkraut
4 Scheiben Ananas
16 dünne Scheiben mageren Räucherspeck oder Dörrfleisch
4 Paar Frankfurter Würstchen

1. Die Zwiebel fein würfeln und in der Butter hellgelb anschwitzen. Sauerkraut, 3 EL Wasser und die geschälten, entkernten und gewürfelten Äpfel zugeben. Ca. 10-15 Minuten kochen lassen, bis die Äpfel verkocht sind.

2. Ananas würfeln und unter das Sauerkraut ziehen.

3. Die Frankfurter mit je 2 Scheiben Räucherspeck umwickeln und auf das Sauerkraut legen. Im geschlossenen Topf ca. 10 Minuten bei geringer Hitze garen lassen. Mit Kartoffelpüree servieren.

Rezept für 4 Personen
Zubereitungsdauer: ca. 30 Minuten

Smoked Bacon Frankfurter Rolls

4 small apples
1 onion
40 g butter
500 g sauerkraut
4 pineapple rings
16 thin slices of smoked lean bacon (or dried meat)
4 pairs of Frankfurter sausages

1. Dice the onion finely and fry in butter until golden. Add the sauerkraut, 3 tbsp water and the peeled, cored and diced apples. Simmer for 10-15 minutes until the apples are completely soft.

2. Dice the pineapples and stir into the sauerkraut.

3. Wrap two pieces of bacon around each Frankfurter and lay on top of the sauerkraut. Cover and simmer for 10 minutes over a low heat. Serve with mashed potatoes.

Serves four, takes about 30 minutes to prepare.

Frankfurter Würstchenspieß auf grünem Erbsbrei

400 g grüne Trockenerbsen
Speckschwarte
2 Zwiebeln
Suppengrün
Majoran
4 Paar Frankfurter Würstchen
200 g magerer Räucherspeck
500 g kleine Kartoffeln
Butter
Salz, Pfeffer
Petersilie

1. Die tags zuvor eingeweichten Erbsen mit der Speckschwarte, Suppengrün, 1 Zwiebel, Majoran und entsprechend Wasser kochen und nach ca. 1 Stunde im Mixer pürieren.

2. Die Würstchen in 3 cm große Stücke schneiden und mit kleinen Scheiben Räucherspeck abwechselnd auf Holzspieße stecken. Die aufgespießten Würstchen kurz von allen Seiten anbraten und auf dem Erbsenbrei anrichten. Mit in Butter goldgelb gebratenen, kleingehackten Zwiebeln garnieren.

3. Die Kartoffeln waschen, schälen und kochen. In Butter schwenken und mit gehackter Petersilie bestreut zu den Spießen servieren.

Rezept für 4 Personen
Zubereitungsdauer: ca. 1 Stunde und 30 Minuten

Frankfurter Kebabs with Pease Pudding

400 g dried green peas
Rind of bacon
2 onions
Soup vegetables
Marjoram
4 pairs of Frankfurter sausages
200 g lean smoked bacon
500 g small potatoes
Butter
Salt, pepper
Parsley

1. Soak the peas overnight. The next day, add the bacon rind, soup vegetables, 1 onion and the marjoram to the peas, add sufficient water and simmer for about one hour. Then liquidize in the mixer.

2. Cut the sausages into 3 cm lengths and spear on wooden skewers, alternating the pieces of sausage with small slices of smoked bacon. Fry the kebabs briefly on all sides and lay on top of the peas. Garnish with chopped onions (fried in butter until golden brown).

3. Wash, peel and boil the potatoes. Roll in butter, garnish with chopped parsley and serve with the kebabs.

Serves four, takes about 1 hour 30 minutes to prepare.

Frankfurter Würstchen-klöße mit Wirsing

700 g Wirsing
800 g Kartoffeln
30 g Speck
1 ½ Zwiebeln
1 Paar Frankfurter Würstchen
125 g Hackfleisch
1 Ei
1 Scheibe Weißbrot
Semmelmehl
1 Tomate
Salz, Pfeffer
Muskat
gehackte Kräuter
30 g Mehl
¼ l Fleischbrühe
3 EL Öl
1 Würfel Bratsoße

1. Kartoffeln waschen, kochen, schälen und in Scheiben schneiden.

2. Den Speck und 1 Zwiebel fein würfeln und in einem großen Topf anschwitzen.

3. Wirsing vom Strunk befreien, klein schneiden und mit etwas Wasser und der Fleischbrühe zu Speck und Zwiebeln geben.

4. Die gegarten Frankfurter in sehr kurze Stücke schneiden und mit dem Hackfleisch, der restlichen, gehackten Zwiebel, der kleingewürfelten Tomate und dem eingeweichten, gut ausgedrückten Weißbrot vermischen. Mit Salz, Pfeffer und Kräutern würzen und das Semmelmehl unterrühren.

5. Die Masse zu runden Klößen formen und 20 Minuten bei geschlossenem Topf auf dem Kohl garen. Herausnehmen, halbieren, auf der gesondert bereiteten Bratensoße anrichten und warm stellen.

6. Die Kartoffeln in eine Pfanne geben und anbraten.

7. Nach dem Herausnehmen der Klöße den Kohl mit Mehl bestreuen, noch einige Minuten durchkochen und mit Salz, Pfeffer und Muskat abschmecken.

Rezept für 4 Personen
Zubereitungsdauer: ca. 40 Minuten

Frankfurter Dumplings with Savoy Cabbage

700 g Savoy cabbage
800 g potatoes
30 bacon
1 ½ onions
1 pair of Frankfurter sausages
125 mince (ground meat)
1 egg
1 slice of white bread
Breadcrumbs
1 tomato
Salt, pepper
Nutmeg
Chopped herbs
30 g flour
¼ l meat stock
3 tbsp oil
1 meat stock (gravy) cube

1. Wash, boil and peel the potatoes and cut into slices.

2. Dice the bacon and one onion finely and fry gently in a large pan.

3. Remove the stalk from the cabbage, chop the cabbage and add to the bacon and onion. Pour on the meat stock and a little water.

4. Soak the white bread and knead to remove excess liquid. Heat the Frankfurters, cut into small pieces and mix with the ground meat, the remaining onion (chopped), the diced tomato and the bread. Season with salt, pepper and herbs and stir in the breadcrumbs.

5. Form round dumplings from this mixture. Put into the pan on top of the cabbage, cover, and cook for 20 minutes. Remove the dumplings from the pan and cut them in half. Prepare the gravy from the stock cube, place dumplings in gravy and put to one side.

6. Brown the potatoes in a pan.

7. Sprinkle the cabbage with flour, allow to simmer for another few minutes and season with salt, pepper and nutmeg.

Serves four, takes about 40 minutes to prepare.

Sauerkraut-Eintopf

500 g Tomaten
4 Paar Frankfurter Würstchen
4 große Zwiebeln
2 EL Schweineschmalz
Salz,
10 Pfefferkörner
1 TL Kümmel
2 Lorbeerblätter
5 Wacholderbeeren
0,1 l helles Bier
0,2 l Fleischbrühe

1. Tomaten schälen und grob schneiden, Würstchen in 1 cm große Stücke schneiden, Zwiebeln schälen und in Ringe schneiden.

2. Schweineschmalz in einer Bratpfanne erhitzen, die Würstchenstücke kurz anbraten, die Zwiebeln hinzugeben und beides goldgelb braten.

3. Tomaten, Wurst und Zwiebeln in einen Topf schichten und mit Salz, Pfefferkörnern, Wacholderbeeren, Kümmel und Lorbeer würzen.

4. Den Bratfond mit dem Bier und der Fleischbrühe vom Boden der Pfanne lösen und dem Wursttopf hinzufügen.

5. Das Ganze 15 Minuten kochen lassen und mit Sauerkraut und Kartoffelpüree servieren.

Rezept für 4 Personen
Zubereitungsdauer: ca. 25 Minuten

Sauerkraut Stew

500 g peeled tomatoes
4 pairs of Frankfurter sausages
4 large onions
2 tbsp pork fat (dripping)
Salt
10 peppercorns
1 tsp caraway
2 bayleaves
5 juniper berries
0.1 l beer (lager)
0.2 l meat stock

1. Peel the tomatoes and cut into large pieces. Cut the sausages into 1 cm slices, peel the onions and cut into rings.

2. Heat the dripping in a frying pan, first fry the sausages in the fat, then add the onions and fry both until golden brown.

3. Put layers of tomato, sausage and onions in a pan, season with salt, peppercorns, juniper berries, caraway and bayleaf.

4. Pour the beer and meat stock into the frying pan, stir to mix in meat solids and juices from the bottom of the pan, and add to the sausage stew.

5. Simmer for 15 minutes and serve with sauerkraut and mashed potatoes.

Serves four, takes about 25 minutes to prepare.

Lauch-Würstchentopf

750 g Lauch
500 g Kartoffeln
4 Paar Frankfurter Würstchen
Salz, Pfeffer
Muskat
¼ l Fleischbrühe

1. Lauch putzen, waschen und in 1 cm große Stücke schneiden. Die Kartoffeln waschen, schälen und in kleine Würfel schneiden.

2. Die Würstchen abwechselnd in einen passenden Topf schichten, jede Schicht mit Salz, Pfeffer und Muskat würzen.

3. Mit Brühe begießen und zugedeckt den Würstchentopf 35-40 Minuten dünsten. Mit Kartoffelpüree servieren.

Rezept für 4 Personen
Zubereitungsdauer: ca. 1 Stunde

Leek and Sausage Stew

750 g leeks
500 g potatoes
4 pairs of Frankfurter sausages
Salt, pepper
Nutmeg
¼ l meat stock

1. Clean and wash the leeks and cut into 1 cm slices. Wash, peel and dice the potatoes.

2. Layer the sausages with the other ingredients in a suitably-sized pan, seasoning each layer with salt, pepper and nutmeg.

3. Pour on the meat stock, cover, and simmer for 35-40 minutes. Serve with mashed potatoes.

Serves four, takes about one hour to prepare.

Der Herausgeber dankt der Direktion und den Mitarbeitern des Steigenberger Frankfurter Hofs, Frankfurt am Main, für ihre wertvolle Zusammenarbeit.

Dank auch den folgenden Institutionen und Personen für ihre Unterstützung:

Stadtarchiv Frankfurt am Main,
Amt für Fremdenverkehr Frankfurt am Main,
Herrn Rigobert Hanauske, Gemaltes Haus, Frankfurt am Main,
Freiherr Johann Philipp von Bethmann,
den Ehefrauen der Mitglieder des Rotary Clubs Bad Homburg v. d. H..

The publisher would like to thank management and staff of Steigenberger Frankfurt, for their valuable assistance in making of this book.

Thanks also to the following institutions and persons for their co-operation:

Stadtarchiv Frankfurt am Main,
Amt für Fremdenverkehr Frankfurt am Main,
Mr. Rigobert Hanauske, Gemaltes Haus, Frankfurt am Main,
Freiherr Johann Philipp von Bethmann,
the spouses of the members of the Rotary Club of Bad Homburg v. d. H..